"A genuine portrait of an African American woman born in Louisiana (the early years), educated in Pennsylvania (the formative years), and continuing her journey in Arizona (adult years). Verilyn Jackson-Downing's sincere reflection of her past delivers. Her narrative provides a glimpse of a Black girl growing into womanhood and the challenges she overcame."

Ollievita Williams, Ed. D.
Educator, Writer, and Creator of the
Award-Winning Magic Hat Storytime

"Verilyn Jackson-Downing is a dear and precious friend of over 20 years. We met and worshipped at the same church in Peoria, Arizona. We have established a priceless and lasting godly friendship. Verilyn laughs easily and listens intently, which makes her an easy, fun-loving person to communicate with. I believe this is due to the life she has lived and the people she has met, compounded by struggles, trials, and tribulations. Her life is a compilation of adversities, pleasures, and joys. Through her story, we see her courage, perseverance, and tenacity. She overcame and is standing strong. Verilyn could and did do all things through Christ, who strengthened her. This book is profound, compelling, and transforming. Her amazing journey will enlighten and encourage you. A must read."

Rose Fairweather
Founder, Destiny Revealed Ministry
Missionary-Evangelist to Belize
Founder, Destiny Preschool, Belize
Founder, Destiny Mentoring Center,
Belize, Central America

UNDERESTIMATED: STILL STANDING!

Getting Through Life's Challenges

VERILYN JACKSON-DOWNING

UNDERESTIMATED: Still Standing!
Getting Through Life's Challenges
Verilyn Jackson-Downing

To contact the author:
verilycanaan@gmail.com

Published by:

Mary Ethel

Mary Ethel Eckard
Frisco, Texas

Library of Congress Control Number: 2025916137
ISBN (Print): 978-1-966561-20-0
ISBN (Hardcover): 978-1-966561-22-4
ISBN (eBook): 978-1-966561-21-7

DEDICATION

In loving memory of my deceased parents.
Thanks, Mom (Louise), for the love you gave.
Thanks, Dad (Sarge), for the love you tried
to give that I refused and miss today.
You both set a standard that continues to inspire me.
I want to make you proud.

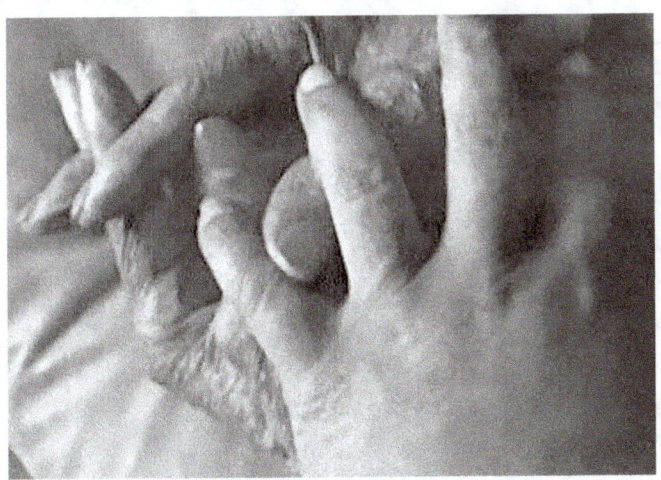

Holding Mom's Hand

ACKNOWLEDGEMENTS

Karen Colbert has been my mentor, friend, accountability partner in writing, and encourager.

Raymond Ferebee, an encourager and friend, helped me find the graphic used on the cover of my book.

Linda Mansfield, my friend with great organizational skills, helped me write my bio and pull together book graphics.

Jennifer Harris introduced me to Mary Ethel Eckard, my editor and publisher, who helped me organize and publish this book.

Robert Riley, a kind soul who gave me space, showed me patience, and has been my encourager.

Thank you to my childhood friends, adult friends, and colleagues for generously sharing your insightful reflections on our past career and relationships. You are all cherished treasures and have left an unforgettable mark on my life that I deeply value. Grateful!

CONTENTS

"*A life is not important except in the impact it has on other lives.*"
Jackie Robinson

"*Act as if what you do makes a difference. It does.*"
William James

"*If only you could sense how important you are to the lives of those you meet; how important you can be to people you may never even dream of. There is something of yourself that you leave meeting the other person.*"
Fred Rogers

"*Maybe I am not an important person in your life. But one day when you hear my name you would just smile and say, 'I had a friend in this name.' That's enough for me….*"
Unknown

PROLOGUE

The number 70 often symbolizes completeness or wholeness, and in that sense, reaching the age of 70 can be seen as a fulfilling milestone. Living beyond 70 is seen as a milestone, a bonus, and a gift of extra time. For those who have reached 70, it's an opportunity to reflect on the fullness of life and to embrace the wisdom that comes with it. I am so glad the Bible doesn't just celebrate the number of years we live but also encourages us to live those years with purpose and faithfulness.

Proverbs 16:31 says,
"Gray hair is a crown of glory; gained in a righteous life."

God is so good to me. I have lived to be 70 plus. None of my 3 siblings are living today. Both parents have transitioned. Occasionally, I experience solitude. I miss that familial closeness and love, especially during holidays. I am sentimental and vulnerable during those periods.

Deuteronomy 31:8 is my favorite Bible verse, my anthem, my mantra. It says,

"The Lord himself goes before you and will be with you; he will never leave you nor forsake you. Do not be afraid; do not be discouraged." NLT

I need to give praise and honor to the true and living God who has kept me, who has watched over me and protected me when I didn't know I needed protection.

One of those remarkable, and dare I say, miraculous times, occurred 12/2009.

A friend and I decided we would meet early at our church, Fresh Start, and help put together bicycles for the children for Christmas. I got up early that morning, dressed, and was on my way to Peoria, Arizona, which was off Thunderbird Road. I had completed writing my Christmas cards to be mailed at the nearby post office off 83rd Avenue, of which I needed to make a left turn. I always took 75th Avenue to Thunderbird Road and then made a right turn onto 83rd Avenue to the church.

Somewhere between making a left turn off 75th onto Thunderbird and getting to the church, I lost consciousness while driving. When I regained consciousness, I was in my car, on the right hand side of Thunderbird Road, just beyond an underpass. I regained consciousness when I heard someone ask, "Are you all right? Are you all right?" I looked and didn't know who they were. I asked, "Who are you?" They continued to ask, "Are you all right?"

I started to open my car door to get out and they said, "Stay in the car. Don't get out. Don't get out." Within seconds, I was in an ambulance and the paramedics were looking me over, taking my vitals, and the police came over to ask me questions, of which I had no answers for.

I looked out the back of the ambulance toward my vehicle to the left. It seemed that I saw and heard two fluttering creatures going back and forth to protect that side of Thunderbird Road where my car, the ambulance, and the police car were parked.

The paramedics told me that my blood pressure was high, and they were taking me to the hospital. I was confused, trying to figure out what was going on. When we arrived, I was admitted and checked into a room. I called my friend to let her know I would not make it to the church. I didn't have much else to tell her because I was waiting to hear.

The nurses came in and checked my vitals. That afternoon, a neurologist came to see me. He was a specialist from India who began asking me questions about what happened. I told him I didn't know; I was driving and then I was in an ambulance. Apparently, he had a little more information and some sense of the power of God, because he again examined me and shared that God was looking after me. I said, "Yes, He always does." He continued, "Miss Downing, from the report of the police, you did not run into a home. You did not run into another car. You are physically okay. But from what I can see, I don't know why you may have had a seizure and no memory of what happened, so God was definitely looking over you." I answered, "Amen."

The hospital held me overnight and allowed me to go home the next day. A friend came to get me, and I asked her to drive by the area where my car was last parked. As we drove by, it seemed like an awfully small area for three vehicles to be parked: my car, the ambulance, and the police car. In my memory, as I was in the ambulance looking out, the area seemed to be extended. I couldn't explain it, and it puzzled me.

I found out that I had only damaged my vehicle on the right front portion around my wheel. It was scraped so, apparently, I hit something during my blackout. Otherwise, the car was drivable. I was grateful that I didn't hurt anyone else, didn't hurt myself, and did not damage any property.

I had driven and made a left turn onto 83rd Avenue to mail the Christmas cards. I came out of the post office driveway and took a left turn onto 83rd at the light, took another left turn, and rather than continuing straight across Thunderbird to the church, I made a left turn and found myself parked just past the underpass, to the right side of the road. That's where God safely parked my car and, I do believe to this day, those fluttering creatures and the other two men asking me if I was okay and instructing me to stay in the car, were angels protecting me and the side of the road where we were. Hearing their voices, I simultaneously awoke.

With the way I was driving during my blackout, there is no way I should be alive. There is no way I should not have caused a fatal accident! How did I not hurt anyone else or cause major damage to my car or someone's home? It is by the mercy and grace of God that I am able to report this miraculous, wonderful, loving power of Jesus who continues to take care of me. I am grateful that He loves me and that He continues to watch over me like the sparrow. Glory to God!

I attempted to find out who helped me get out of the car. I called the ambulance service and the police, but they didn't have any reports of witnesses. I knew there were two or three fluttering beings going back and forth, protecting all of us.

It was a miracle. The wonderful, spiritually divine protection of Almighty God protecting and keeping me. To this day, I do not have residual memory or brain issues except for the normal ones that old age brings. What a wonderful gift. I am so grateful to God.

"We are spiritual beings having a human experience."
Teilhard de Chardin/Wayne Dyer

I am writing this brief memoir to share my dream of self-realization and to inspire others to be resilient and to love themself and others in this journey called life.

May we never forget how far God has taken us within our sphere of influence!

Always be grateful.

My 70th Birthday Celebration

INTRODUCTION

January 14, 2022. Today is the first day this writer actually began to manifest content for her story about the adventurous women who decided to find a career in the Department of Corrections - SCI CAMP HILL PRISON (SCIC).

Sci Camp Hill was and still is a prison in Camp Hill (Cumberland County), Pennsylvania, designed to hold men. It was opened in 1941 as the Industrial School at White Hill for young offenders. In 1975, it was ruled that SCI Camp Hill was not an appropriate place to house juvenile offenders, and in 1977, the institution began housing adult male offenders. It now serves as the state's sole diagnostic and classification center for men and houses adult male offenders.

From mid-1984 into the 1990s, it was a low to medium level prison. The Camp Hill State Prison is currently a level 4 correctional facility.

April 13, 2022. In January, I contacted elementary school friends and other staff that I worked with at SCIC, but I didn't receive much feedback. So, I scrapped that plan and decided to write about my life / my memoir which would include a few highlights of my career in State Corrections and my journey through life.

In hesitancy and procrastination, I formulated how to start and who to contact. I wondered if I really had anything to say, and I wanted feedback from others. I required a mirror to show me parts of my early life because, during those days, I felt invisible, like a shadow, and not important.

In 2023, my mentor, Karen C., advised me, "Just write. Don't worry about specifics. The hard part is to put the time in and write. I started writing in 2023 after her encouragement. She kept me accountable. With a smile, she would question, "How are you doing? Have you been writing?" She shared that it took her several years to finish her book, and I thought maybe I could do that too.

As a child, I always had a knowing within my spirit that I am meant to do something important. I hope this doesn't sound arrogant or grandiose. In my small mind, I couldn't see how God was going to do it. Or maybe it was not for me to figure out or know exactly what it would be. But, as they say, time waits for no one. Time keeps on rolling, rolling along. Only God knows the end from the beginning. So intermittently, I would sit and write my story. And through the writing, God continued to confirm through others that I was to keep writing.

Isaiah 46:10 NIV says,
"I make known the end from the beginning, from ancient times, what is to come. I say, 'My purpose will stand, and I will do all that I please.'"

On December 26, 2024, the day after Christmas, Robert, my boyfriend, called his Aunt Sarah. She did not know me. When we shared my name, she had difficulty pronouncing it. When she pronounced it correctly (Ver i lyn), she said "That's a unique name." She then said, "I think that name is unique, and it'll be on a book." I was sitting alongside Robert when she shared this, and I spoke that goosebumps had raised on my arms. I asked, "Are you prophesying that I will have my name on a book?" Then I said to her, "Wow, this is really wild because I have started writing a book." She said, "Don't let nothing stop you because God is going to bless you. Keep doing what you're doing."

As of March 5, 2025, some SCIC staff agreed to share their perspectives with me about the women who first started working inside the prison. There were women who held important positions in personnel / HR, the records office, and teachers who came in and out of the prison.

Around and about 1983, the first two female officers (COs) were hired to work directly in population with the inmates. One was Sargeant Ruth R. Some consider her the GOAT OF FEMALE OFFICERS. Other comments include "an awesome person to work with," "She had a heart of gold," "Enjoyed working with her," "She was the best," and "She worked in A block and was promoted to other positions within the all-adult male prison." The second female officer was Ms. Johnette "Billy" Kennedy. Officer Kennedy worked in block A and H. I never got a chance to meet Officer Kennedy but knew of her. I give these women much respect for initiating a righteous reputation and cracking the ceiling / opening for other women to follow.

In March 1984, I came aboard as the first Black and first female Correctional Activities Specialist in the state of Pennsylvania to work directly with the male inmates in population.

We three were the originals at SCIC. Many other women came aboard after a couple of years. To name a few, there was Ms. Flowers who worked in G block and RHU, B. Ewan, K. Wilson, R. Rutter, James, D. Johnson, T. Smith, Lt. Whitehead, Zobitne, and V. Morris.

Some male officers have commented it was wonderful working with strong women who were fair and knew the job, while there were other men who did not feel or believe that women should be working directly with the inmate population and didn't appreciate the positive standard women were setting. Some officers were very critical, at times, and made it a tough reality for the women working inside.

Nevertheless, it has been my supreme pleasure and privilege to have worked with the women and men at SCIC back in the day. Pennsylvania State Corrections has been very good to me.

Bravo to all the women!

CHAPTER 1

Let's Begin

If you're gonna start a story, you might as well start at the beginning. At first, I considered writing about my years in the field of corrections because I used to journal my experiences. However, some of my precious written memories and pictures were discarded, due to life events and situations.[1]

This book is based on highlights of my past; my memoir, if you please. Many people have prophesied over my life, and many have been right on point / correct. God has wonderfully given me dreams as well. My memory has faded, but I still recall the vivid parts. So, let's begin.

I grew up down South, in Mansfield, Louisiana, as a nappy head Black girl riding my bike, barefooted, and playing with my friends along the dusty red dirt roads. We would pick fresh fruits and berries anytime of the day when they were in season. It was summertime and it was hot and humid. There were small homes, nicely kept, by no means poor, but by no means rich. We had extra land on the side of our little house surrounded by many neighbors. We were country folks and self-sufficient, for the most part.

Our church in Louisiana, known as True Vine Baptist, was the family church. It was in the country, meaning deep in the southern woods.

We visited our Grannie who lived very simply, and we enjoyed hanging out with our first cousins who also lived there. We all had nicknames. My sister, Carol, was called Black gal, my older brother's nickname, Al, was a shortened version of his real name, Alfred, and my nickname was Nanny Newt. Somewhere over time, it became just Nanny, and my younger brother was Jay. Our primary cousins' nicknames were Squirrel, Sonny, and Ray.

We had the best of living. No cares, no electricity, no running water. We went to the spring to collect water or we used filtered rainwater. There was an outhouse, we had to milk the cows, churn the butter, slop the pigs, feed the chickens and gather eggs, and wash clothes in a big black pot outside over the fire. Grannie made the soap and hung the clothes on the clothesline to dry in the fresh sunshine. We plowed our fields, and we ate fresh fruit and vegetables daily. Grannie made our bed mattresses out of mounds and mounds of feathers; we slept 3-4 in one bed.

On Saturday night, we would get our baths in a tub after the water was heated on the wood stove. Two or three kids got a bath in the same bath water; we just added more fresh water to what was already there. Then, depending on the seasons, we would sit in front of the big old fireplace, talking and smelling the sweet pine wood burning while we had a snack and watched the crackling fire before bedtime. To this day, one of my favorite things is the smell of a woodburning fireplace. My mind immediately takes me back to those sweet, treasured memories.

We woke up early to do our chores as assigned and then came into the house to a plate of fresh eggs, bacon or sausage, grits, homemade biscuits with syrup, and some buttermilk. Boy, that's what you call good eating. Then we would go play in the woods and creeks catching crawfish, playing hide and go seek, and cowboys and Indians.

At the crack of dawn, early Sunday, we would get up to do chores, eat a hearty breakfast, and get ready for church. Sunday morning, the prayers were prayed, the hymns sung, the preacher preached, the choir sang, the Holy Ghost reigned down, and the saints were happy! I was able to imitate my granny when she got happy and caught the Spirit. We went to church all day Sunday, had our picnics with our baskets of fried chicken, cornbread, potato salad, fresh slices of bread, iced tea, lemonade, and good times. Then we went back to church for evening service. Those were the best childhood times.

We lived in a close knit area on Shallowhorn Street in a thriving segregated neighborhood with schools, businesses, and other things necessary for living. It was the early 1960s and no one was talking about integrating neighborhoods. As a matter of fact, I rarely had contact with Whites unless we went downtown to shop.

I had lots of good friends. We played from early in the morning till dusk, and then we had to be in the house. My mother was always a good mother. Mostly she was alone as my father was in the military, and he was often away. My mother worked and maintained four children very nicely when we lived in Louisiana. We attended church and we grew up in church, and Mom held true to Christian values. She was neither a curser, a yeller, or a permissive-type parent, nor was my dad. Mom made sure we dressed appropriately, as if we were a reflection of her. She always said, "You may not have what other kids have, but you can still be clean and look good."

Mom was limited in her compliments toward us kids, but we knew when she was proud of us and, Lord God, we knew when she was mad as hell. She did not spare the rod, although she wasn't abusive. I think I got one whipping from Mom, and my sister got a couple more than me, for me. And Dad was no joke. He whooped us harder than Mom. He had that military, slave kinda, discipline thing going on. He would put us on his knees and give us a few slashes with a belt with holes in it. We all learned quickly to obey our dad. Nobody wanted that kind of whipping.

Our brother, Al, got into trouble more than any of us. Al got his last whipping when he was 16 years old. I cried for him. I would be the first to cry for any sibling who was getting a whipping, even if we were all in trouble.

I was the one told to be quiet, although I wasn't much of a talker. I was sensitive, and my sister seemed to be more protective of me in our childhood. I was also criticized more because, in my sister's view, Mom didn't make me do much around the house. I was sicklier with sore tonsils, anemia, and such. During periods of illness, I was permitted to sleep with my mother more frequently than my siblings.

Mom kept herself snatched and looking good. She kept us clean and happy, she kept us fed; in my mind, we didn't want for anything except waiting eagerly, impatiently, when our dad would come home with gifts for each of us. The four of us had to present our report cards to him so that he would know we were learning in school. He needed to have a measure of our progress because education was important to him, as a young Black man, who went into the military early. (He changed his age to go into the military.)

We always heard that mantra, "Get your education, get your education," so we had to perform not only in school but in many other ways.

When my two older siblings were able to go to school, the first day was exciting. They got cleaned up in their new school clothes with a good straight press of their hair or new haircuts, wearing their new socks and shoes, and off they went to learn.

In our single level home, we had a picture window in the front room. On the first day of school, being the third of four children, I watched my brother and sister leave. My brother, Al, was four years older than me, and my sister, Carol, was three years older. I would observe them departing for school, eagerly and joyfully greeting their friends along the road as they walked to school. I stood in the picture window so excited and ready to go learn.

I couldn't wait to start school. And then, the day came for me to enter elementary school. I was excited to get my new clothes, shoes, and hair styled for 1st grade. We met all the other children outside of our house as we headed to school in an all-black, segregated neighborhood. We were all Blacks walking to school together, laughing at and with each other.

My first-grade teacher, Miss Williams, was (and is) an important role model and figure. Why? I just loved her, she was so nice, and we seemed to learn what we needed to learn. I felt safe and secure at school. No thoughts of fear, hurt, harm or danger, just excitement. There was no need to worry about being called any names, being bullied or being hurt. I could be myself as I was -- a little Black girl with a good mom and dad, good brothers and sister, and good friends who enjoyed the warm, hot, sweaty Louisiana sunshine. School was a good time.

The lessons I learned would be taught early in life, mostly by my dad who came in and out with his progressive changes in how he wanted his children to respond in life and to others. Dad's homecoming, his military visits, were always something I looked forward to. I remember him saying to us with gifts in hand, "You are no better than anyone else and no one else is any better than you."

He taught us to answer with respect to our elders. We didn't have to always say yes ma'am or sir or no ma'am or sir. We were able to say yes and no when appropriate. I absorbed those experiences, allowing them to permeate my mind, body, and spirit.

When I was a young child growing up in Mansfield, LA, I was excited to see my dad with his uniform starched and pressed and looking so handsome and dignified. I was proud of him. But he could be a tough character at times because he expected a lot from us, and we chose to perform and do the best we could for him.

One of those time happened in the fall when I was 5-6 years old. We were slaughtering a pig on our property. During the slaughtering, everyone pitched in to do whatever was asked. Dad asked me to bring a bucket of hot water to an adult. The water had been poured into the bucket, and I was told to be careful. I was dressed in an outfit of long blue jeans, pants, and a blouse. As I walked, the water was slushing around, and I somehow slipped. My right knee went into the scalding hot water. Yelling and crying in pain, my mom caught me up in her arms and drove feverishly to the local hospital. I was in shock from the pain. After cutting off the pants on the right side of my jeans, the doctors said I had third degree burns from my upper thigh to halfway down my calf.

While the doctors were working on me, my primary concern was that the doctors not mess up my panties. This was one of those home-grown things Mama used to say to her girls regarding hygiene. We were taught to change our underwear daily. "Keep on clean underwear because you never know when you might need to go to the hospital."

I had two skin drafts on my leg. When doctors saw it, they commented that it healed very well. It is funny how and when home training shows up during desperate times. I was embarrassed when I was much younger, and it negatively affected my self-esteem. Today I have the scar on my leg, and it is just another reminder that I am unique. Often people think it is a birthmark, but I know it's my angel kiss. God was gracious enough to save my leg and keep it useful.

This was just one of many ways and times He would show up throughout my lifetime to hold me, save me, protect me, and comfort me. **I was learning to harness my God-strength to carry me through the days.**

Young Verilyn in Grade School

My Mom, Louise, in Her Younger Years

My Mom, Louise

My Dad, Sarge

CHAPTER 2

⤛⦿⤜

Life in the Bubble

During these years, we lived in a safe and happy bubble. In our Black neighborhood, my siblings and I, along with our friends, frequented department stores, barbecue shops, gas stations, and ice cream stores through the front doors. We were confident, loved, and unafraid to enjoy life. We liked our dill pickles with peppermint sticks in them, and we liked the penny candy and pickled pigs' feet, and we loved our barbecue restaurants with the delicious smells wafting in and around the shop.

Our Christmases always seemed magical. We didn't have much, but at the same time, we had a lot. We had a Black Santa Claus and a Christmas tree. Mom would provide practical gifts like new clothes, mostly underwear. She said, "People always need good, clean underwear and good, clean socks. Give those things because they are the most valuable."[2]

We would share our gifts lists, and we often received gifts that we wanted, like new bikes or shoes, along with bunches of Christmas striped sweet candies, round, hard, oblong, squared candies, and lots of fresh fruits and nuts in our little bags. We got our own little red netted Christmas stocking bags. It was something we delighted in, and we would squeak and clap with happiness. We would be so happy to have our own little collection and treasure these things. We could eat them at our leisure, at our pleasure, and brag about how much we got amongst ourselves and our friends.

Then we would go outside and shoot off fireworks while holding the firecrackers. We learned to light them in our own hands and throw them. They would burst, snap and pop, and boom. The sparklers were lit in our hands, or we would stick them in the ground. We would squeal and laugh with our neighbors and our friends. We were happy to be able to do that.

It was a great time in the neighborhood. We planted vegetables on the plot of land beside our house. We had great, kind, fun, neighbors. We could go out my back door and holler at Miss Emma and we could crisscross between property lines; there were no fences.

We briefly used the outhouses, which were not a pleasurable experience, but they were a necessity. In some way, somehow, Mom and Dad managed to get plumbing and running water into our little house. We had one bathroom for our family of six, but it was so much better than having to use the unpleasant outhouse.

We were a middle class Black family and we lived well, maybe even better than some of our neighbors. Our house was always painted, and my mom made sure we kept it up and clean. She worked hard for us, and she always looked beautiful.

When my dad came home, the bedroom doors were always shut. We would secretly giggle, hearing them having sex late at night when we had to go down the hall to the bathroom. We were sure to bypass their bedroom by going through the kitchen and the living room to get to the bathroom.

My sister and I shared a bedroom, and my two brothers shared a bedroom. We had a black and white TV in the living room where we watched cartoons, Laurel and Hardy, The 3 Stooges, Disney, Lawrence Welk, animal shows, Stepin Fetchit, and all the other Negro shows presented to us.

Sometimes Dad would put us in the car, and we would learn to drive on the dirt roads. My older sister and brother said they had driven Dad to and from the bars without their licenses, but we lived in an agricultural farm town so there were a lot of back roads they could take. My mom knew about it, but she knew Dad was safe and was teaching them how to drive.

I'm Too Young for This

Our friends lived close by, and it was nothing to stay overnight with them. One week when I was six, I stayed overnight at a friend's house who lived behind us. There wasn't always room in the home to have separate beds, so I slept with my friend's older sister. I had slept over before with no problems, and we all knew each other. But things happened gradually and, before I knew it, I was involved in something I didn't invite.

This older sister, who was also a friend of my older sister, began to caress me. At first it was on my back and, eventually, she turned me toward her and began to caress the front of my body, down to my private parts. I was not sure what to do or feel, however my body enjoyed the caresses and the hands of the older female friend. This was my first illicit sexual encounter. I was told not to tell anyone because it was our secret, so, I went along with this on a few occasions until the sexual encounters got to the level of rubbing and dry humping.

There were times I was sore in my private parts, but I kept it secret. The last time I engaged sexually with the older friend, I told myself, "If this is all sex is, it isn't for me." After that, I avoided staying overnight at my friend's house and I also avoided her older sister. Later I came to realize that I had been groomed and sexually molested by a female. I shared this with my older sister, and she was shocked and angered that her friend had done this to me.

I questioned myself as to what I had learned from this experience. I told myself,

"YOU CAN'T TRUST EVERYONE.
YOU NEED TO TAKE CARE OF YOURSELF."

And I reminded myself,

"MY BODY IS MY BODY,
AND NO ONE CAN DO WHAT THEY
WANT WITH MY BODY."

I learned my body does like to be loved, and touch is very powerful. Secrets can be hurtful and dangerous to keep. Was I traumatized? I wasn't impressed with having sex with a girl, if that was all that would happen: rubbing, dry humping, and being sore in and around my private parts for days. It made bike riding very uncomfortable.

Upon my later reflection of this illicit sexual encounter, emotionally, I didn't feel that I was traumatized, but I knew it wasn't right to do again. And I warned others of the things people might try to do to little kids.

Leaving the Bubble

When we left the bubble of Shallowhorn Street to go shopping or to explore, things were different. There was an intrinsic sense of needing to protect ourselves and abide by the rules that we weren't familiar with or sure of. We were with the white people and had to move to the side of the walkway as they walked toward and past us. We had to go to the back windows of the ice cream parlor to get our ice cream (at the *colored only* window). We could only drink at the *colored* water fountain. Those were times when I had questions in my mind, in my spirit, and in my soul. My dad would say, "You're no better than anyone else, and no one is better than you." I wondered about this treatment of white people acting better than black people, and I kept this growing, repressed anger inside, never really to be spoken, but only felt and suppressed.

I was happy to get back to our own neighborhood and stores where we could go through the front doors to get what we wanted and happily run out. We preferred the safety of our Black community, but that wouldn't last. We were told that we would be integrated, and that was a big word for us.

Being integrated meant that we would be going to school with white kids. I heard the words but didn't understand or grasp what that would mean for me. I knew it would be different, and I shared all this with my friends. We weren't sure if we were looking forward to it. We just knew it was something that was going to be happening. In the meantime, we had our bikes, our dogs, our homes, our friends, and we kept playing, not worrying about tomorrow.

Sometime in 1963 or 64, our parents informed us that we needed to leave Louisiana and, of course, we were wondering what was going on? Mom explained that our dad was leaving the military and, after 20 years of service, this would be the first time for them to have day to day, 24 hours each day, and 365 days each year, to be together and gain knowledge of each other. We were going to be a family with two parents and four kids, and Dad wanted to move to Pennsylvania to do that. I couldn't remember where Pennsylvania was, but we all knew it was up North.

The move meant we had to work a little bit harder, particularly in our education, even before we moved. The people up North in Pennsylvania were a little bit smarter than the people down South in Louisiana. My parents encouraged us to work hard in school, so we put extra special effort into our studies. When we presented our report cards, the one with the most A's got the first choice of gifts that Dad would bring home for us as a reward. He was proud that we were working harder in school.

Mom began getting things ready to move. I wasn't sure how I felt because I was happy in Louisiana. But this was a new day. Things were exciting! Eventually, a big truck drove up in front of our house, and my mom said it was a moving truck. A moving truck? Oh, wait! We had to get all of our furniture into this big truck. We had to pack and move quickly. Mom and the men carried out everything as she had packed it. We had basic things we put in our car for the drive to Pennsylvania. Things were happening so quickly, I cannot remember what I was feeling.

Then we were on the road to Pennsylvania. Dad was wearing civilian clothes. We were dressed comfortably, the four kids and our parents, as we headed north. Of course, along the highway we would pull off to the side so Dad could get gas. We didn't know anything about a green book or places we needed to stop to be safe. Those things were kept from us. Only adults knew about those. When we needed to use the bathroom, we would stop along the road. When we were hungry, we would have a picnic of chicken, fruits, vegetables and lemonade or water, and then hurry through the next town or state as we headed north.

I slept on and off as we drove, and then I heard, "We are in Pennsylvania." I was 7 or 8 years old when we pulled into Shippensburg, PA. When we arrived at our street, it was nighttime, but it wasn't dark-dark. We passed three houses before we got to ours, which was almost like a haunted house. It was huge with two stories, and it had a wraparound porch. There was one more big house to the left of ours, and they were all made in the same style and had two stories.

I heard the disappointment in Mom's voice as she let out a gasp and asked, "You brought us to this?" Dad didn't say anything. I don't know what description he had given to my mom along the way as to what we were coming to, but somehow it wasn't what she had pictured. She was disappointed. Our house in Louisiana was one-floor with three bedrooms, a kitchen, living room, and a bathroom. This house was in enough repair that we could go inside, but it wasn't quite what Mom was expecting. Somehow, in the blur of my memories, it got fixed up enough to make it acceptable to her.

Dad had to go to work at Letterkenny Army Depot in Chambersburg, about 11 miles from our home. We had to get registered for school and were given pep talks as to how things were gonna be a little different and how to set our expectations. You know military style (strict / structured) and, of course, we were ready to perform and do our best to please our parents. Dad was a retired staff sergeant in the military, known as "Sarge." My mom had gotten some college education in nursing. Financially, with her career skills, Dad's job and his military pension, we lived well in the middle class.

In Shippensburg, the kids' bedrooms were upstairs. We weren't used to stairs, up and down, up and down. My brothers' bedroom was across from us, and downstairs was our parents' bedroom, the living room, dining room, and kitchen. We had about a quarter of an acre of land in the back of our house, and we had to work hard to get it in shape. The front yard was enough to mow, and we had a paved street in front of our house that led to nowhere.

Across the street was farmland with lots of cows and a creek with trees that shielded the land from our front porch. We had no garage or driveway, but we had a shed we could park under. My siblings and I would often sit on the porch and take it all in. It was a quiet, beautiful, calming area.

I did not know what was in store for the family, except for cleaning up our house and yard area to get them suitable for Mom and Dad. We were in full "all hands-on deck" mode. A few days after we arrived, the moving truck came, and moving people began to unload our furniture into our home. I had a feeling that things were going to be new and different.

Mom and Kids in Louisiana

CHAPTER 3

Acclimating

Everyone could see they had a new family on the street. I met the kids who lived on Brookside Avenue and the girls who lived up the road. Somehow, we started playing, and we would get laughed at because of our southern accent and how we would say things, like "Can you *tote* this?" We called our shoes "*tennis shoes,*" and they called them "*sneakers.*" I would be like, "What the heck? These are our tennis shoes!" and they thought that was the most hilarious thing.

We had to learn to use a fork rather than a spoon, and our friends called the evening meal *dinner*, while we called it *supper*. We had our southern twang on things. I don't think it was malicious teasing, but we were teased and laughed at, and we were able to laugh with it. I thank God for our father and mother who taught us enough to be confident and somewhat secure in ourselves, to not only be laughed at but to be able to laugh with others about ourselves.

Quiet as it was kept, my new friends were the ones with the strange way of pronouncing words. We were all able to make friends, and we did a lot of the things in Pennsylvania that we did down South. But we didn't run barefoot in Pennsylvania, even though the summers were wonderful. We wore our *tennis shoes*.

In the group of girls I ran around with, there was a hierarchy. There was Sherri, Sal, Deb, and a girl, Evita, who came during the summer to stay with her grandma, who lived in the house next to a little dirt road. We were not sure what was down that road, and our parents wouldn't allow us to check it out. We knew to follow their rules and obey their words. My friends and I rode our bikes up and down the road we lived on, and we played jump rope and hide and go seek in my back yard.

Mom drove me to my first day of school at Roland Laboratory Elementary, which was an all-white school. My first experience was one of feeling fear as I walked through the school and saw all the white kids headed toward their classrooms. Nobody looked like me. Mom introduced me to the white teacher, who introduced me to the class. I wanted to hide behind my mother's skirt. There was a sea of white faces looking at me, and nobody looked like me.

The teacher said, "We need to put our new student at a desk." No one had preassigned me a desk, which would have sent the message, "Here is your place that you belong. This is your safe spot." Those minutes seemed like hours before someone said, "Oh, she can sit beside me, here at this desk." Her name was Mary W. My heart seemed to happily fly away for that moment, as it seemed I was accepted. I went to my little desk and, eventually, I did acclimate to school. I had a couple of friends who treated me like I had always been treated.

School was a distance away, so after the first day, we had to ride the school bus. And when we got home, Dad was very strict in what we were to do first. He was right about our studies and he made sure we weren't held back from our grade level. My math was not up to par with the kids in Pennsylvania. Dad recognized that quickly, so we had big old poster boards with the timetable on them. One of the things we had to do each day after school was to read and practice our multiplication table.

Over time, my friends understood what the expectations were for the Canaan children. One lifelong friend today, Evita, would come to Shippensburg during the summer months from Chambersburg and we could not go out to play until we had studied our math/multiplication table. So she either studied with us or had to leave until we were done.[3]

Below are excerpts from elementary and high school classmates and colleagues.

Email received from Connie J. on August 24, 2024

> *Hey Verilyn,*
>
> *I have often thought about you and where you may be. I remember we were best friends in grade school. I didn't think about your color, and I don't remember when it occurred to me that you were Black. Probably when my parents would not allow me to invite you to my house to play. My parents were very prejudiced, though I am happy to say that I never felt that way. People are all the same in my opinion. Some are good and some are not so good, no matter what color.*
>
> *I considered you a very dear friend and I don't take that lightly. Real friendship just clicks*

between two people, and it is not easily found. I am happy to know you are in this world somewhere. Thank you for the gift of getting in touch.

Email received from June M. on August 15, 2024

Dear Verilyn,

From the time I met you in elementary school, I was drawn to your sweet, kind nature. You made me feel happy, because it was easy to make you smile, and you were always ready and willing to play together. You were never mean, never a bully, like some others.

You told me once that you were scared when you came to Rowland Lab. That surprised me because you always seemed so outgoing. Way more than I was. For that fear that you felt as a little, innocent girl, I am so sorry.

If I had known how you felt, I surely would have hugged you so tightly. It may not have made it go away, but at least you would have known that I cared, and that you had someone on your team.

You said that being Black and coming to a White school was very intimidating. I could never know what that felt like, but I came from a large, white family, a poor family, or so I thought then. Yes, we lived in a crowded, little house, and wore hand me downs from cousins, and Mom and Dad bought clothes from the neighbors for my brothers that their son had outgrown. So, I was intimidated, in a different way. Never feeling like I measured up with the "rich" kids with their new lunch boxes and matching thermos, new clothes and shoes, store bought white bread, often with Lebanon bologna, while I had homemade bread or wheat bread in a brown recycled ice cream bag. Never feeling like I was good enough.

But, when a little girl named Verilyn came to our class, instantly, we were friends and playmates. I looked forward to recess to be with you. Always smiling and happy. I felt worthy, good enough to be a friend, and didn't feel judged.

Junior High came and brought so many changes, and we never got to be together, only in passing, and the same thing in high school. We made lots of new friends. I always had Holly and Connie. But, when we grew up, their parents changed a lot of our being together. We became adults and contacted each other and got together to talk about the past. We were able to do pretty much what you and I are doing now, vent and reminisce, only we didn't write a book, which we surely could and probably should!

Even though we went our own way in life, you are still that girl who is always smiling, always lighthearted and fun, always making me feel happy to be around you. Those are my thoughts and feelings when I think of you. That is what you represent to me. Happy, light-hearted, fun, a good person, and a good friend.

Rowland Lab Elementary in Shippensburg, PA

CHAPTER 4

Family Life in Pennsylvania

In Pennsylvania, the trees turned colors to beautiful reds, oranges, and yellows. It was warm but not as hot and humid as Louisiana. There were not many Black people in Shippensburg, but we were surrounded by agriculture, and farmers were all around us, which was familiar.

When we sat on that wrap around porch, we watched people drive by. Jay and I would have fly killing games to see who could kill the most flies. The big ol mountains in the distance stood magnificently in all their thick greenery. I often wondered how hard it must have been for the covered wagons to cross over those bad boys back in the day.

Shippensburg was a very serene, safe town to live in. We weren't friends of cats, but we had pets as we did down south, which were usually dogs. I always had a dog that stayed outside and ate dog food with an occasional scrap of human food.

We were able to run around during the summer months and go anywhere we wanted, but we had to be home by dusk. We had lights on our street, so in the evenings, we played near home, under the lights and sang the Beatles songs like we were the band. "He loves me yeah, yeah, yeah!"[4] We didn't always lock our doors at home; we just closed them.

My dad couldn't mow the backyard properly without danger from the many stones that would be flying out from under the lawnmower. It was our job to line up in the backyard and go step-by-step, picking up big stones, for whatever length of time, so my dad would be able to safely mow. And that's what we did. If our friends wanted to play or be with us, they were also lined up, going step by step, picking up stones and putting them in a bag. This is another one of the famous stories about my family told by Evita. At some point after clearing the stones and rocks out of the backyard, we plowed the ground and planted our little garden.

My mom enjoyed our friends coming over, and she often joked and laughed with them. She enjoyed cooking for them, and she was a firm believer in not eating in front of people if we didn't have enough to share, and at that point, we would postpone dinner until they left.

Everybody respected my mom and my dad amongst the other adult Blacks, and the Black kids had a healthy fear (respect) for my parents as well. They knew how strict they were, and nobody wanted trouble with Mr. or Mrs. Canaan.

Christmas remained a happy and joyous time for our family. We were initially enthralled about all the snow in the wintertime. We shoveled the snow, made snow angels, had snowball fights, and played until our fingers and feet were so cold they felt numb. To get warm by the coal furnace, we pushed and shoved each other to stand over the heating grates. We stripped out of our wet, cold clothes and looked forward to hot chocolate.

Mom and Dad had to purchase lots of coal. My brother, Al, and Dad were responsible for going to the dank, dark basement and shoveling coal into the furnace. Sometimes us girls would accompany our brother and play around in the basement where Mom also kept her canned jars of vegetables and fruit harvested from our yard and garden.

My brother, Al, was a jokester. He was popular, athletic, handsome, good at sports, and liked the ladies. Everybody wanted to be around Al. When he was in high school, someone threw a rock, and it hit him in the eye. He lost the eye, and the military provided great health benefits for military kids, so he went to another state to get a glass eye so he wouldn't stand out. He wore a patch for a short period of time until his glass eye was ready. Sometimes he would use the glass eye to scare people or to be the center of attention.

My sister, Carol, was the parentified, second mother of the house. That was her role early on in life, to take care of us, to cook, and to help clean. As a young girl, Carol had lighter skin patches around her eyes. They were very noticeable because she was a beautiful, dark skinned, melanated, girl. No one could explain why the lighter skin patches were there. As she got older and into adulthood, she began having more health symptoms. After many years of medical testing, it was diagnosed as Lupus, which is an autoimmune disease and runs throughout our family.

My little brother and I were close at that time, and he was nonchalant and more reserved. He was only a year younger, and he was Dad's favorite. Jay was quiet, he did what he needed to do, and that was that. There is a song that says still waters run deep. That's my song for him.

Dad had expectations for Jay to play baseball because my dad played baseball in the military. We all knew he loved baseball because we had to watch baseball constantly. Because Jay was the youngest, he had more quality time with Dad upon his retirement from the Army. Jay was into little league baseball, so there was a natural closeness in their relationship. He was also an avid reader. Both he and Al were two who knew a little about everything but were masters at none.

One of our big summer vacation trips was going to Philadelphia to visit the Connie Mack baseball stadium (21st Street and W. Lehigh). Boring. My older brother, Al, was good at sports as well, but Dad doted on Jay because he had more time to spend with him. Al sought and wanted the love and approval of Dad, but he didn't have the time with Dad that Jay had.[5]

As for me, during my first years in Shippensburg, I felt the cultural shock of being in a new place, but I kept it to myself. I was somewhat sensitive, shy, invisible and felt emotionally numb, like I was the middle kid. I played, I smiled at school, and then I went home. This time period was a scary blur, but I survived it. I was the crybaby of the family, the invisible one; the middle child in terms of roles. Why? My siblings seemed to have their own identity, but I felt like I was a shell of a person. I didn't have parental attention, so at home, I was able to get away and not be made to do things. I was muted and out of people's way. Still to this day, my philosophy is "lead, follow, or get out of the way." That's probably why, as I grew and matured, I came up with the idea to become a "city girl" who was outgoing, bold, and someone special. More on that later.

I grew more mature and mentally conscious in the middle school years, which is just that rite of passage for most kids. I was trying to figure out who I am and what I'm about. In my middle school graduating class of 1967, I wasn't popular, but neither was I a cast off; I just didn't realize it. I would hang around, observing, feeling, listening, and having fun while padding my way through.

Finding Our Church

Dad was not a church goer, but he enjoyed listening to Gospel music, and he never stopped us from attending services. Mom took us kids to an African Methodist Episcopal Church (AME). We eventually visited the Baptist church in Chambersburg, but it was too far to travel every Sunday. We ended up staying at the AME with the few Black people who were in Shippensburg.

It was not what we were used to. The service was dry and structured. It was a quiet church, everybody sat nodding, there were some quiet amens spoken and the quiet clapping of hands. Even still, we had to be involved in church. We were active in the children's services, Sunday school, ushering and singing in the choir, but it lacked the spirit, enthusiasm, and the glory I was accustomed to.

I wanted to understand for myself what the Spirit of the Lord was all about. I was running the streets in the small town of Shippensburg with my friends. We were stealing fruit off trees, knocking on doors and running away from people as they yelled at us. My friends and I were not criminally bad kids, we were just mischievous. We would pick fresh berries whenever in season. And wherever we could, we would go into the farmland or walk in the creek.

We had our little girl's group and eventually we became a little gang, The Black Diamonds. We would get into the pastures where the bulls were, and we would try to make the bulls come after us (like bull fighters) and dodge them. Then we would run outside the fence as quickly as we could, and we would laugh and frolic. Evita made herself the leader. I considered myself the unspoken second in command and then the rest of the girls were members of the gang. Evita was the fastest runner, and I was the second fastest. In my mind, I think that's kind of how we chose leaders.

Evita "E" would come to Shippensburg in the summertime, which is when we had our gang meetings. One summer, we went into the forbidden area, which was beside the dirt road with the little wooded area past the fourth house on our street. We made our way through the bushes and the trees, and when we saw a big tree, we hung a tire swing and would swing across the creek. That was our hiding place, our secret fun area. I remember having one fight with E. She threw mud on my white sweater, and we went at it. Our angry feelings didn't last long, and we played together the next day.

I went to Chambersburg to do a sleepover with Evita and her mom, Ms. Jane, who was kind and strict with E. I was a little jealous of my friend because she went to ballet classes, and I wanted to go to ballet classes. My mom said we couldn't afford ballet classes, which disappointed me. I kept those feelings to myself. I was getting good at storing up disappointment, anger, and feelings of being invisible. Soon, that would all come to a head. But not yet.

CHAPTER 5

Childhood Traditions

My dad loved to drink alcohol, and he had lots of buddies. Most times he did not do his socializing in Shippensburg. He went to Chambersburg where his work buddies, hunting buddies, and other buddies were on the weekends. He would come home around two or three o'clock in the morning. My mom, being a dutiful wife, would be awake and the whole house would be awakened. When he came home from drinking and partying with his friends, he would often bring people with him, usually his buddies, and they would sit in the living room.

Oh, my goodness! When the music on the reel to reel started, it seemed it would play forever. He also had a record player, and he would play the music loud. His favorite song was *"When a man loves a woman."* At some point, whether early in the morning or late at night, that song would be played. By that time, the whole house was awake, and my mom was making breakfast. We would stumble and bumble down the steps and be called into the room to sing or to express an opinion about the meaning of the lyrics of another song Dad was playing. And, of course, we had to be introduced. These people must have forgotten our names, because we were introduced almost every time. He would go down the line of who we were, his kids, and he loved to say our names and share us with his friends.

As I think back, I believe he wanted to show his buddies how educated we were, because that reflected on him. We did our best, of course, because we wanted to please him and we wanted to show off. I also think we wanted to please and impress him and his friends, and then we would be allowed to go back to bed or to get dressed and do whatever we had to do for that day. Once the performance was over and they were fed, Dad's friends would stumble out and go home, and Dad would head to the bedroom to sleep it off.[6] As a child, I consciously did not choose to harbor negative feelings about Dad's drunken privacy violations and weekend demands for performances. [7]

Dad enjoyed deer hunting with his friends, and Pennsylvania is a big hunting state. After he shot a deer, he wasn't sure how to carve it or prepare it, so he called some friends over. We had a deep freezer, and we kept it stocked with a variety of meats like venison, beef, and pork. The freezer was also stocked with vegetables from our garden and ice cream.

We learned to be proper northerners eating with a fork, not a spoon or with our hands, while eating greens and cornbread. Mom was a great cook and made the best biscuits and homemade desserts. We could count on beautiful, wonderful desserts after meals and for the holidays. Dad's favorite joke after meals would be his response when we asked, "What's for dessert?" He would respond with a big ole grin, "You all can dessert the table."

The only time Mom drank alcohol was during holiday dinners. She would pull out a bottle of Morgan David red wine. It was a sweet wine; not too bitter and nasty. That was the only time the kids would have alcohol. My sister was not a drinker, but my brothers drank theirs, and my sister would often give her glass of wine to me. I was anemic and had my tonsils removed, but I was told that Morgan David was good for anemia, so that was my justification. It was good childhood fun, lifetime memories, and tradition.

Another childhood tradition Dad implemented was family court. Although he had an authoritarian parenting style, he would hold court before we were punished for any wrongdoing. "Hear ye, hear ye, the court is now in session." Dad, of course, was the judge. The individual was able to make their case in regard to disobedience to said rules. The jury was the rest of the family. Everyone could state their opinion on what the issue was and state the level of punishment they thought fit the crime. Dad had the last word. "So said the Judge." We also had family meetings to discuss things so that we would be on the same page.

We acclimated to integration, but because we watched television, we knew we were in the middle of a tumultuous scene for civil rights. My mom had her pictures of Martin Luther King, Kennedy, and Jesus Christ on the walls. I remember the days King and Kennedy were assassinated. There was chaos in the schools with the news blasting, and we heard rumors spreading like wildfire that both men had been killed and there were fights and protests down South and around the United States.

Philadelphia and Pittsburgh had protests, but in our little, sheltered town of Shippensburg, there was no protest amongst the few Blacks who lived there. We had only four Black people in my graduating class. On television, it was crazy in the big cities, but amongst the Blacks who were in Shippensburg, we knew what was going on and our issues were minor.

Because we lived in a college town, students came from other places with racist attitudes. Racist students would call us the N- word. My older brother and sister would come home and talk about how they were called names (the N- word) and they had to fight with the white boys from the college. I didn't experience anyone calling me that while living there. I did not have to get off the sidewalk when Whites were passing. I was treated pretty much equally in those situations, even when I went downtown.

The parades were a big thing in Shippensburg, and everyone knew about it. The different families of Blacks, who lived in different areas of Shippensburg, gathered on one corner on Main Street downtown, and we had a good time. Our family lived in Pumpkin Center and the other Blacks lived in Pussy Harbor, with a few scattered in between. We knew we would either meet at the corner on parade day or at church. We were able to greet each other and enjoy downtown together and go to the soda shop.

The parades were long and boring for me, coming from down South. In Louisiana, we were used to bands coming down the street, playing upbeat music, with the majorettes strutting their stuff, kicking high, and throwing their batons. Each band would stop and do a little dance or performance to get everybody clapping, yelling, and screaming, while beautifully dressed in their uniforms. That was always a good time from those high school and middle school bands back down South.

In the North, we had a couple of bands, and the one from Shippensburg played sad music during their parade march. It sounded good, but it was nothing that would excite young people or make us want to dance and enjoy the performance.

The bands didn't stop to perform or do dance moves. Then there were tractors, trailers, fire trucks, and ambulances. I thought, "Oh, alright, really, this is it?" But it gave us an excuse to go downtown and meet in the center of the city.

After the parade, the adults would go into the bars and us kids would make our way somewhere to hang out. We would laugh, joke, tease each other, sit in the yard for the rest of the afternoon and, of course, be home by dusk before the streetlights came on.

Those were good times. Had we known that our world was going to drastically change, maybe we would have relished the days a little more.

CHAPTER 6

Dark Days and Regrets

On one of my dad's weekend trips to Chambersburg, he was in a car accident. He had been drinking. My mom went to check on him. He had a DUI and was in the hospital for about two weeks, but eventually he came home. Mom had to go to work, so the kids took shifts to help care for him, bring him food, and do whatever he and Mom needed from us.

After a couple of weeks, Dad was not doing well, and Mom called the ambulance. Dad was taken to Chambersburg, which was 11 miles away. I don't remember visiting him in the hospital. They eventually took him to Walter Reed Army Medical Center in Washington, DC for treatment. Mom took off work to care for him, and we went to school to keep up with our studies.

When I was in the 8th grade, I was called to the school office. I don't remember whether I was told at home or at school, but I remember the words, "Sarge has passed. Your dad has passed. He is dead." He died from a blood clot in the brain, and we kids did not get a chance to say our goodbyes, and I did not get a chance to tell him that I loved him.

All I could say was, "Well I didn't, I couldn't..." There were lots of things in my head, but I didn't know how to express what was in my heart. I had so many questions. "Well, what time?" "Where?" "How" "What happened?" "How can he be dead?" "We're just getting to know him and to live with him. He can't be gone!" "What are we gonna do?"

Those were the things in my head. I didn't get it. I didn't get a chance to see him, to say goodbye. We had an estranged and complicated relationship in those few years before he died in 1966. We only had five to six years to be with him full-time. Dad exemplified a strong work ethic, even during those times and those drunken weekends. My experience was trying to love him in person. I was still trying to get to know him. I can't say what it was for my sister. Her relationship with him was hard to read. She was a part-time mom to us and, believe me, she let us know that later in life. My older brother, Al, of course, was doing his thing. He was out of the house playing sports or socializing with his friends.

As his youngest daughter, I was more protected, and he was stricter with me and my sister. On occasions, he did try to have a nurturing and affectionate relationship with me. He would call me and say, "Come here, Verilyn." I would go and he would say, "Give me a hug." I may have had some punishing resentment for him and/or some unsolicited loyalty to and for my mom. She never spoke badly about him, but I knew there were things going on between them. We witnessed a physical fight and, of course, we took sides and tried to protect Mom. She was not a pushover; we didn't have to give her much help.

One time she picked up a few accessible wooden items in the living room and let Dad have it. He soon left the house for a while. I chalked my resentment up as "You're hurting my mom and you're not being nice to her, so you don't get to love me."

Viewing the experience in my child's mind, it was twisted and mixed up, but I wanted to know him. I wanted Dad to love me. I needed him to love me. I just wasn't sure how to love him, and I kept an emotional and physical distance. I was confused, so I often never got the warmth, the tightness from a hug, or the love and affection from my dad. It was an awful time. I felt somewhat lost, scared, and sad. I had a sense of longing. An unrequited love relationship with my dad lingered in my spirit, but I suppressed these feelings.

He was taken to Mansfield, Louisiana for the funeral and burial. We flew down South to his funeral, which was a blur, where the family sat up front and was greeted and offered condolences and sympathies on the passing of Sarge. It was an open casket. Upon final rounds to see the body, I was bewildered, afraid, and had anxiety and grief. As I hesitantly walked toward his casket, I saw his face and wondered, "What did they do to him?" He did not look like himself. How could this be my dad? When I saw the casket go into the ground, I knew whoever was in the casket was gone forever, dead. It may have been some kind of denial because, even at the time, I felt there was still more he and I needed to work out in our conflicted relationship. Now it would not happen.

With my dad gone, I changed, and things around the house changed. We continued going through the motions of life, not stopping to look at the damage or trying to work through the issues. Our finances were also impacted.

Mom had to ration everything, including the coal drops during the winter. Therefore, the thermostat was kept low as she tried to afford the higher price of the coal shipment.

During these times, we would run down the stairs with most of our clothes in our hands and maneuver to be first to the bathroom to put our school clothes on while standing over a heating grate.

In hindsight, I blame the twisted loyalty, resentments, hurt, and unforgiveness, which I could not identify at the time, that kept me at a distance from the love Dad was willing to give to his second daughter.

My only dead father. I do regret holding on to the hurt and pain. I have grieved this over the years. I have apologized to my inner child and have asked Dad to forgive me many times in my prayers. I have done the emotional work to forgive and to give myself grace as I thought and acted as a child. I know that I will see him again in the spirit and look forward to that blessed day when we meet again with the tightest of hugs, with love and peace in our hearts. As an adult I craved his love in my spirit, and I blame myself, but I also recognized and accepted that he was a functional alcoholic.

What I resisted as a child deeply saddens me as an adult and how it has played out in my adult relationships into the emotional deficits and physical contact with a man. I had so much inner child work to reconcile my behavior, my spiritual self, my emotions, and the loss of nurturing from my dad and how this impacted my future relationship with men.

But as an 8th grader, these things were not yet clear to me. I was struggling to find my place and make my own way, and life continued.

CHAPTER 7

My Teen Years

There were many lessons to be learned in my teen years. Many dreams to be had. I wrote in my diary of how I wanted things to be when I dreamed. I wrote the names of my children. I only wanted two. I had a name for my girl, Danielle, but I did not or could not come up with a name for a boy that I really liked. I also dreamed about the life and friends I wanted in high school, who I wanted to date, my life after graduation, what I wanted to become, and how I could better myself to be that person. My dreams seemed bigger than life.

My boyfriends were mostly limited to the few Black boys in the towns of Shippensburg, Chambersburg, and Carlisle. There were 2-4 families of mostly boys and 2-4 different families that were mostly girls. We all grew up liking or going with each other and looking for fresh faces in close surrounding towns. Of course, my brothers were in that pool of possible boyfriends: In Shippensburg, there was the Canaan's, Thomson's, Nacho's, Berk's, Jonson's, and a few other stray Black boys.

Some friends and I would often go to Chambersburg to seek other pools of Black boys, to date, to hang out with, or to go to parties. Carlisle was another town about 22 miles north of us.

The Canaan's learned to drive soon after, if not before, age 16. Because Mom and Dad had always been adamant about us learning to take care of our vehicle and being safe, we were given basic tips on changing the oil so we didn't kill the engine, keeping air in the tires, changing a flat tire, filling the radiator, and keeping a quarter around so we could call for help. This training helped us feel safe when we took off to other places.

We drove farm tractors and, when we lived in the South, Dad taught us to drive on the dirt roads. We did drivers education in high school to help with insurance purposes and to get formal driving instructions and rules of the highway. We were fortunate to each have old hoopties to drive. We worked and earned the money to pay for them. I was able to get my old hoopty from Military support money when Dad passed.

We would often go to these two towns to look for new blood. There was a teen canteen in Shippensburg which was a social event for teenagers on the weekend. All the teens came to dance, Blacks and Whites from all over. Mom was strict with both of us girls. My sister and brother went to the dances, and I couldn't go because I was not old enough. So, I might as well be back at the picture window watching the older kids go have fun.

I turned 13 years old and lots of girls my age were going to the teen canteen and talking about it, and I was always listening. Mom would not let me go for some reason. Then, after I pleaded and begged her to let me go, my sister was a chaperone. And if she was able to go, she was happy with that. I hung out with my friends who were there, dancing and sweating, dancing and sweating, until it was time to go home. It was such fun.

I looked forward to returning to the teen canteen the next weekend. I became more interested in boys, although I was very shy. We often met boys in neighboring towns, and I had a couple of boyfriends from Chambersburg and Carlisle.

When we were all teenagers, Mom often worked into the evenings, and we would party in our community, known as Pumpkin Center. We would chill the bottles of Rolling Rock in the farmers' creek across the street and drink the cool beer or hang out at our house. But we were careful not to cause damage to the furniture or anything in the house. Before Mom would get home, we had everything back in place. This didn't happen often, but kids will be kids.

Mom seemed to work longer and harder hours. The house was quieter on the weekends as Dad was not there to bring his drunken buddies over in the early morning and get us to perform. No gospel music on Sunday mornings. We were even more focused on schoolwork, sports, chores, and establishing individual personalities.

As I entered Shippensburg High School (1967-68), Al entered his senior year. Al always was the center of attention, very good in sports even with one eye. He was good in mathematics, and he was a fun-loving, fast driving jokester and quite a lover of girls. He always had a speed racer type car and flew up and down the highways between home and the closest town. He would bring friends home and Mom always cooked enough food for guests, if Al hadn't raided the refrigeration the night before. It was an exciting year for him, and we were very proud of him graduating.

Carol made a name for herself as she was quite the homemaker and student in high school. She was well-liked and talented in sports, cooking, and sewing like Mom. She became more like a second mom to us after Daddy died. She had her one and only boyfriend whom I was assigned to chaperone on dates, whether it was in our living room watching TV or on dates when they left the house. I got to eat very well during my chaperone days.

My mom was strict, but when teenagers want to get time to themselves, they will find a way. My sister got pregnant in her last year of high school. The whole house was in an uproar. My mom was livid because she felt this was a reflection on her. She ran a tight ship with chaperoning and godly values. Mom made it clear to my sister that this was her baby, and my sister was to be responsible.

We walked around on eggshells for at least a year. Mom clearly stated if we were grown enough to lay down and get pregnant then we were grown enough to take care of the child. Mom was adamant about that, and Carol had to work hard to get back into Mom's good graces. Mom mellowed some during the pregnancy and helped to buy necessary items the baby would need. The teen dad was brought into the picture and given the same responsibility speech and told he would toe the line and help out.

By the time my nephew was born, we were happy with the addition of the family. He was like having a little brother in the house. My sister, Carol, graduated from high school, even after being pregnant.

I pride myself in learning from others behavior. I have a lower tolerance for pain, and I didn't want to repeat something that was going to hurt me. A lesson was observed and learned during this tumultuous period.

Like Mom said, "Keep your legs closed and your panties up."

CHAPTER 8

High School Days

My entrance into high school was exciting and I looked forward to blossoming physically in sports and emotionally. I also liked to read, dance, and play sports, and I was more confident playing intramural sports. I never thought I was very funny, but somehow, I made my friends laugh without being a buffoon.

I had several boyfriends in my high school years. I really liked Stevie a lot and we went together for several years on and off. When the song "Me and Mrs. Jones" comes on, I am instantly reminded of him. I think my family had a thing with his family as my older brother went with his older sister and I was friends with both his sisters at one point. He was also my first heterosexual relationship as a teenager just before heading out to college. He used protection. I also found out that I preferred boys rather than girls. There was more to this thing called sex than rubbing up next to another girl.

As a teenager, Stevie was a smoker and could blow wonderful smoke circles, and he had a great imagination. We had lots of good conversations. He became a marijuana smoker while we were together, which led into an addictive lifestyle of hard drugs. Later in life, he died of a drug overdose. That was a painful time.

I could count my teen boyfriends on one hand. There was another boyfriend who went to a local college and partied; he was shot to death at one of those parties. Short lived relationship. Another boyfriend from the Carlisle area went into the military. He returned only to die from an illness as a young adult.

The Dream: To Get Back to My Roots

My dad and mom had instilled in us to be better than they were. I was concerned about how to do it and be better, wondering what my strengths and talents were. I kept these self-esteem issues to myself. In addition, moving from Louisiana to Shippensburg was a culture shock and I wanted to get back to my culture. I knew I wanted to go to college.

I went to the high school guidance counselor's office and was asked why I wanted to go to a Historical Black College University (HBCU). I shared my views of getting back to my culture and my roots. This college was accredited and offered courses for the career I was interested in.

Three years later, I graduated from high school and secured my entrance into HBCU. I was the first of my siblings to go to college. I wasn't sure what career I would enter. I just knew I was good at sports so I would start there. I was excited and my family was too.

The "Shippensburg experience" had given me a conservative perspective of college life and life in general, even though

I wanted more. I couldn't wait to be a city girl. To grow stronger/courageous, wiser, street-smart, to be a bit of a mouthy extrovert, and to have a fun personality. I wanted to be able to take care of myself and improve my self-esteem. My next four years at college would provide the experience and opportunities I needed to learn how to navigate life on my own.

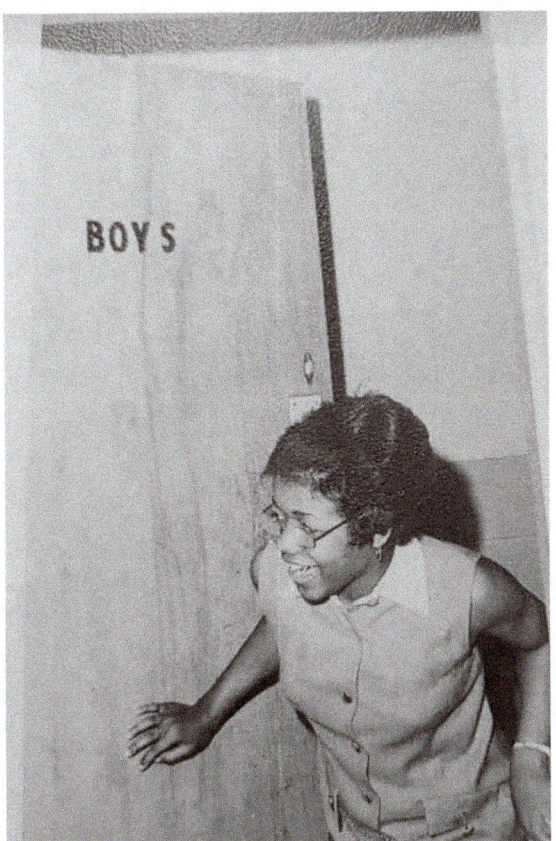

Checking out the Boys Bathroom

CHAPTER 9

Life on Campus

As a 5-foot-statured woman, I dressed conservatively for my first day of college. I had straightened hair that was turned under in a pageboy. I was dressed in a white blouse and a blue "A" line skirt below my knees, with my blue suede buck loafer shoes.

My mom, my sister, and I entered the Cheyney campus. There were lots of cars and families present, with students directing traffic to guide people to their dorms. We were going to Robinson Hall and were directed where to park to unload. Then we found my room.

My roommate was not there but had unloaded her luggage, and her stuff was everywhere. I began to choose a side of the room when my roommate came, and I had my first eye opening experience on the first day of college. I was unprepared for who I thought would be my roommate. We were a shocking contrast of each other. She was about 6 feet tall, thin, light brown skinned, curly hair, and she was wearing a raggedy pair of cut off Daisy Duke shorts and a halter top! She was very outgoing, warm, open, and friendly. Introductions were made and she offered to help me get settled. I didn't have as much as she had, so I kindly said, "No thank you." My family called me by my nickname, Nanny. She heard them and, from that point, I was forever known at college by that name.

Great friendships were formed among about 10+ young women who lived in the surrounding dorm rooms.[8] We laughed, cried, studied, and partied together. We had much the same values and desire to complete college successfully, make the honor roll, and conduct ourselves appropriately, for the most part. We were in most cases the first-generation college graduates in our families, and we called ourselves "The Ladies of Robinson Hall." We were not about to waste our parents' money and expectations on unnecessary bullsh_i_t. I, personally, had a healthy fear of Louise, my mother.

Initially, I thought of becoming a physical therapist. I checked out the classes and thought not. A recreational / gym teacher would work.

Among the many varied life changing experiences were had at Cheyney, one stands out as the most profound. I was in psychology class and the syllabus was distributed. The professor asked if there were questions. He clearly announced in his classroom that he doesn't hold students' hands, and we needed to be sure to follow dates and expectations on the syllabus.

I went back to my dorm room and was mad at myself, as I was unsure of the expectations on the syllabus. I had frozen in the classroom and was scared to ask. I couldn't sleep that night and thought I was getting off to a horrible start in my self-improvement and boosting my self-esteem and the like. Something needed to change, and I needed to be bold to ask even the questions nobody else asked, even if they were dumb questions. I no longer wanted to be in this scary, indecisive place, neither psychologically nor emotionally. **I was determined to summon my God-strength and fear no man.** The only answer the professor could give me was yes, no, or maybe so. He would either answer my question so I could be clear or not answer my question.

The next day of class, I raised my hand and asked a couple of questions for clarification. The professor answered them, and I knew what was expected of me to satisfy the professor and get a good grade. I was proud of myself. Several students thanked me for getting the clarifications as they had been confused also. From this point onward, my approach / my MO was to seek clarification whenever I was uncertain.

This represents a significant behavioral, emotional, and psychological change for me. Now, if something is unclear, I ask for it to be explained in simple terms *that a 6th grader would understand*, as in the movie *"Philadelphia,"* starring Denzel Washington. I am grateful for this practice. **I must summon my God-strength to move me forward to make the next decision or take the next step.**

I loved this psychology Professor. His class opened me to my family dysfunction and family dynamic and provided many personal answers emotionally and mentally. Revelations were waiting to emerge in my development as a young adult who needed to address and heal inner childhood issues. I was excited daily to get to this class and complete extra reading assignments. He invited his students to his home at the end of the semester for a formal dinner mixer. I felt so grown up and was on my best social behavior. It was a great experience. This class solidified my desire to take more psychological classes. I felt like I had found the beginning of my passion for my path to a career. The idea of being able to help myself and help others was so delicious to me. I learned the difference between being assertive versus aggressive.

"To the world you may be one person;
but to one person you may be the world." Dr. Seuss

We dorm friends were like a box of chocolate. We came in all sizes and sweet chocolate complexions, attitudes and personalities. We came from big cities, small towns and the Virgin Islands. I soon had to shake the conservative shy girl persona. I needed to get with my desired bold city girl attitude. In our dorm, we coordinated décor each year, got in each other's business, knew each other boyfriends, sneaked the boys into the dorm rooms, pledged social clubs and sororities, had our chick fights, and still supported each other in any way we could. We discovered the creative, sports, academic, sexual, and social aspects of ourselves. And we did all manner of independent things that I thought I was grown up enough to do. Partying, pledging, weed-smoking, and new sexual experiences. But Lord, no stealing. I did not want to have to face my mother or get kicked out of college. The shame of it all! And I had to maintain the Canaan name.

And I discovered a bold voice that would erupt into rage and anger in social settings. When out, I would take unnecessary risks when I deemed someone was disrespecting me or my person. If I was at a show and seated and someone would stand in front of me, I would get up, tell them to move, and it was not in a kind tone. It was more like an order. And, of course, they would move or somewhat challenge me verbally. It didn't matter how big or small, man or woman.

At a night club with my friends, dancing in close quarters, if someone stepped on my foot, elbowed me, flipped hair in my face, especially Whites, when I brought it to their attention and there was no apology or polite manner to acknowledge my message, it was on! My friends began to ask me, "Do we have to fight tonight if we go out?" I kind of realized there were deep-seated issues that needed to be addressed, and the anger pattern became obvious. But it would take time.

Later I met an upper-class boy at Cheyney and wanted to explore the sexual side of relationships. I had gained some wisdom from my sister's situation and wanted to avoid the wrath of Mom like the plague. Neither was I ready to have my life limited by having a baby.

When I went home from college, I wanted to get birth control pills. I asked Mom for her permission, yet I knew the plan was to be proactive and get to Planned Parenthood as soon as possible. Basically, I was low key informing her that I was going to be sexually active. She asked me why? I explained that I prefer to be safe than sorry. I learned from my sister's previous pregnancy situation. No other response from her. My MO surfaced in this situation. No verbal response meant I could make and follow up on my own decision.

"We are never, ever alone. God is
listening, ready to rescue you."
Psalm 34:17 The Message

I met my first long-term, serious boyfriend (Dave) in the gym. He received a scholarship to play football. He was just a little bit taller than me, and I am only 5 feet tall. He was fun sized just for me. He had the best deep, hearty, loud laugh. The kind that makes you laugh with him, not at him. He was built like a manly brick house. He was muscular in all the right places and had playful eyes. I daydreamed about being Mrs. Dave, but we only lasted for a while after college.

I was a gym rat because my major was Recreation. I met my good friend, Shar, in the gym as she was there to get her degree. Her long-term dream was to own a dance studio. Shar was a non-traditional student, meaning she did not come right out of high school to college. She was a single mother.

Here's what Shar shares about the three of us meeting and connecting in the gym. *"One of my most memorable moments with Dave was asking him if I could pay him $0.50 to squeeze one of his biceps. They were huge for such a little guy. His reaction was a big smile followed by a hearty laugh."* In my years at Cheyney, this person was and still is a significant friend and confidant to me.

I played varsity volleyball and did weight training, as I was skinny for many years. People would tease me about my skinny legs, which I was also ashamed of in high school. At the time, the now famous coach Vivien S. was a professor and she was the women's volleyball and basketball coach at Cheyney.

Some got involved with the lightweight alcohol and herb (marijuana) side of things experimentally. I had access to my car off and on campus, and we traveled from state to state because the drinking age varied by location. We partied and, yes, we had some close calls. Prayer and Jesus were still part of my life mantra during my college years, and I am thankful He saved us from many situations.

I never knew hunger until I was a college student, and I didn't eat chicken wings at home because there was hardly any meat on them. But when I was in college, I was hungry at night, money was short, and they were selling wings at the social café, 4 for a dollar. I scraped up every penny I could find to purchase fried chicken wings. After I ate the meat, I sucked the bones. I looked for a job after classes, learned how to make Ramen Noodles on a hotplate, and added vegetables in that bowl. Life was still good, and I was grateful. You know they say the Lord protects babies and fools.

"His eye is on the sparrow, and I know He watches me."
Matthew 6:25

Below is an email I received from Betty A. with her reflections on campus life at Cheyney State College from 1973-1975. This email was dated 9/14/2024.

For my dear friend Verilyn (Nanny) Canaan Jackson-Downing,

When I first attended Cheyney State College in 1973, I had one childhood friend on campus and she was a mutual friend, Marsenia B.

Verilyn, you were introduced to me by my friend Senia as "Nanny," which was a name given to you by your family. You became one of my dear friends on campus. I truly appreciated your kindness, energy, positive attitude, and most important wisdom. This was my first time away from home in West Philadelphia living in a Christian household where I was very sheltered to the ways of social life and activities.

Nanny, I always admired your socialization skills and laughter which made me feel very comfortable in your company with our dorm mates. Nanny, you encouraged me to speak up and to show up, especially at a few of those campus dances. You taught me how to dance, and you also taught me to have confidence in my abilities with other people and friends living on campus and Tubman Hall.

Another exciting time that I'll never forget was traveling on the Cheyney State College bus to a men's basketball game at Shippensburg State College. This is your hometown where your family lives. It was agreed we had to go meet your mama. We girls left the college bus and went to your mama's house. We were so excited and loved meeting her. She greeted us with a big smile while we introduced ourselves. Your mama was so warm and hospitable towards us, and she just made us feel like we were at home.

I'll never forget your mother's kindness. Yes, clearly you have your mother's kind ways and that's why we continue to call you Nanny. You were the one, Verilyn, who always kept the joy in the room filled with laughter! I always felt your warm sisterly friendship. I lovingly embrace you. Thank you, my sister!

In that Cheyney spirit and love,
Bettie A. 1976
Cheyney Alumni Life Member

"But thanks be to God!
He gives us the victory through our Lord Jesus Christ."
1 Corinthians 15:57 NIV

Verilyn with Cheyney Friends

Verilyn and Ollievita

Varsity Volleyball with Coach Vivian Stringer

**After all these years, this group of friends from
Cheyney's Robinson Hall is still together**

CHAPTER 10

Challenges, Careers, and Changes

You are on purpose!
You are right where God wants you to be.
God has great plans for you!

"For I know the plans I have for you," says the Lord.
"They are plans for good…. To give you a future and a hope."
Jeremiah 29:11 NLT

I graduated from Cheyney University in 1975 with my BS and
city girl bold attitude. I was more self-confident and ready to
start my life. I went to work in Germantown, Philadelphia at
the YWCA as an aerobics instructor. My long-term boyfriend,
Dave, chose to marry a White girl, but we remained friends.[9]

I lived and worked in Germantown for two years. I had
friends who were caring, a bit older, and more experienced.
I was never turned out, out of control, or let anyone control

me, and I was able to be less conservative and open to letting my hair down and trying new sexual things.

Due to lack of grant funding for the YWCA, my position was not renewed so I returned to Shippensburg. I lived with my mom and helped her at home while also working in manufacturing at the Pennsylvania Glass Plant, which was in Carlisle. I was of petite stature, yet physically and athletically strong. I was teased about being small, but I was able to lift the large plates of glass from the rolling belt line and carry them to the packaging box. I got it done, albeit the muscles in my body were screaming in pain.

For about six months, I commuted to Carlisle to work with eight or so friends. We enjoyed being together and building new relationships, some platonic and others romantic. An unlikely relationship was with one of the Thomson boys. He was cute, but I was not his fast-girl type. I thought of myself as sheltered, average, and not very attractive. I wasn't ugly; I had a descent body build yet with dang skinny legs. He also knew how strict my Mom, Louise, was, as his brother was my brother-in-law.

As young adults, we kept our casual relationship under wraps by going to movies and eating out. When he moved to Carlisle, our rendezvous took place in his apartment. As quiet as it was kept and being from a small town, folks knew about us. At one point, we were teased that I might become the second Canaan family member to marry into their family. I became acquainted to a very different side of his public personality, which was boisterous and extroverted. When we were alone together, I enjoyed the humor, care, and intimate moments we shared.

I soon grew tired of being in Shippensburg and desired another move in my career, another adventure to see the world. I also had this angst inside to honor my father in some small way. My older brother could not enter the military due to his missing eye, and my younger brother wasn't interested in the military, though he did eventually go into the army, keeping our family military legacy intact.

In my mind, the military and its discipline benefits had played a significant and positive role in my overall life. There seemed to be more advantages than disadvantages to getting ahead. I could go into the military as an officer with my college degree and I could travel the world. (I was too short to fulfill my other dream, which was being an airline stewardess.) I could honor my father and continue the legacy of serving our country as he and several of my uncles had done, while also making a good life for my future family.

I determined the military would be the thing to do. I wanted to look sharp in my uniform; I wanted to get the highest degree of respect as a woman in the military. I saw on the commercials the Marines were looking for a few good men. Well, they were also looking for me …. one of a few good women. I chose the Marines! Semper Fi!

Upon entering the Marines, I was put on delayed entry and did not leave for Camp Lejeune, South Carolina for approximately 3 months. Basic training was fun, and I was excited to be challenged and prove my worth. I learned to make my bed so a coin could pop up, take care of my clothing, and weapon assembly and care. I was given the nickname of "slug" because I was leaning on the door frame in our unit when a female drill sergeant came by.

In 1977, women ate in separate areas of the mess hall from the males, and we learned to get in formation to march to the mess hall, around base, during drills, etc. I was getting into the swing of the scheduling and discipline of basic training, often comforting young 18-year-olds who cried and wailed because of homesickness. There were a couple who decided this was not the life for them and they quit the military.

I was counting the days in basic training and knew I had approximately 2 months and one wake up left. I was looking to get my stripe as a corporal upon graduation. One night, I didn't feel so well. Something was different but I was not sick. I let this go on for approximately a week. Then, I decided to go to sick call, shared some of my symptoms, and took a pee test. Medics didn't find anything medically wrong with me. So, I continued my training.

Within a few days, I was called into the Commanding Officer's office and given the news that I was pregnant. (In hindsight, I could have waited until after graduation to get checked out.) What a surprise and a hot mess. I needed to pack my things and move to the unit where outgoing people lived until they were discharged from the military. I was also told I could reenlist after having the baby, but I would need to go through Basic Training again.

I was in a bit of shock. It hit me, and my decision-making process and plans for my future were in jeopardy. This is where my sadness, disappointment and irresponsibility to take proper care during my previous sexual experiences came upon me. I had been careful to take birth control pills in a timely manner, or so I thought.

I mourned the fact that I was not able to keep my family legacy of military service intact, putting a hitch in my career / retirement, seeing the world, and getting paid to do it. During out-processing, I was responsible for the women being discharged in my unit. I became their faux drill sergeant for all movement in and around the base. Though I didn't realize it at the time, God would use this experience as a drill sergeant in my career in the coming years. He doesn't waste anything.

After I was discharged, I flew into Philadelphia and talked to my friend, Shar, who was a treasure and support. We talked seriously about my situation. I chose not to reach out to the father. I did not want to interrupt his small-town life and complicate my decision. I was selfish and self-caring at the same time. I could hear my mother saying, "If you are grown enough to lay down and get pregnant, then be grown enough to take care of it." I knew I didn't have a lot of time to quibble over what I needed to do. I cried and prayed over my decision to abort the baby, asking God for forgiveness for what I was about to do. Spiritually, I knew I was killing a baby, and I knew this was not what I was taught to do. Then, cold-steeled and determined to move on with my life, I set up the appointment with the clinic. Prior to the procedure, I was counseled, but then I went through with my decision.

I returned to Shippensburg. Who says you can never go home? I began applying for jobs with the railroad and the state of PA. I worked at the railroad in Pennsylvania for a year as a clerk, which means I had to join the union and complete assignments from substituting for vacationing office clerks (who would ask for me anytime they went on vacation) to cleaning bathrooms. My mama always said if the job was legal, then do a good job. I wasn't too crazy about cleaning, but I cleaned the bathrooms while holding my breath or putting perfume on a mask. I comforted myself with the thought that I was getting paid doggone good to clean.

After the first year as a clerk, I started on the third shift. I walked miles at night in the cold to reconcile the numbers on the freight cars with the printout sheets. This is when I got pay differential, which was more money hourly.

I also drove the jitney for the drunken conductors and engineers. When these men were picked up to go get breakfast and then taken back to the train for their shift, it surprised, dare I say, startled them, that a woman sat in the driver's seat. They did not respect that women could do almost anything they could do and be good at it. I proved them wrong and received compliments for my driving. We enjoyed teasing and harassing each other. I also met wonderful friends there who became lifetime friends until they passed into eternal life.

While on the third shift, I also learned to get power naps for 15-20 minute periods while the men were eating breakfast at Denny's. They would invite me to go inside with them, but I would turn them down so I could sleep. I thought it might take me about 45 minutes to fall asleep, but I was wrong. Because I was tired and opportunities to sleep were not often available, I learned quickly to shut down hard and fast so I could be refreshed.

After-Effects of the Abortion

Since the time of the abortion, I told the potential father about the decision I had made, and I asked God multiple times for forgiveness. I have often had thoughts about the gender of my child and how my life may have been different had I kept the baby. I do not wallow in those thoughts or feelings. However, spiritually, I believe and relish the thought that this sweet soul will meet me in the spiritual realm. Amen.

When I have been confronted with another woman's decision about having an abortion, I have prayed with them and shared my belief that it is a sin, yet it is their decision and they will need to deal with God about their decision at their judgment. Even though I made the decision to have an abortion, I no longer condone that decision. But I also don't judge those who have or who will choose to do that.

I read something on Facebook that seemed to be just for me from my baby.

> *"Hi Verilyn! It's your little one. Even though I am far away, in a place beyond your sight, I want you to feel my presence beside you. I've made my home in the skies above, wrapped in love and warmth. Whenever you miss me, just look up at the stars. I'll be one of them."*

Eventually, life led me to Harrisburg, PA where I moved in temporarily with my sister and her husband. I was still looking for the job that would get me the best benefits for retirement and challenge me in professional growth.

Verilyn in Grade School and at 44

Carol and her husband, Terry

CHAPTER 11

The Cheshire Cat and the Chain Breaker

While I was living with my sister and brother-in-law, my college degree was useful in helping Carol get certified in her daycare business. After a year, I wanted to get my career started and get a job in my educated field. I put in applications with the state for jobs in the recreational/forestry field. I wanted a state or federal job for the long-term benefits they offered, like retirement, more equal pay, good vacation and personal time off, and the ability to be upwardly mobile.

Around this time, I realized that I was not satisfied with my life. I was beginning to think the weed was making me forget things and I needed to make a change. My sister had become a Jehovah's Witness, and she would bug me until I decided to study under them, as they seemed to have more cognitive knowledge about the Bible, thus spiritual knowledge. I thought they could help to make sense of the scriptures and the inconsistencies, the fantasy and fables in the Bible.

Jehovah's Witness was helping me make sense of some concepts, however, one of the things I did not like was that they exiled people for any deemed sins the church didn't like. Jesus was not their savior, and I didn't like thinking I could be exiled, even though the Bible teaches about forgiveness. They also had weird rules about health concerns, they went door to door with their doctrine, and they did not visit other denominations who believed in Jesus.

As I was learning about Jehovah's Witness and waiting for the perfect job, I did odd jobs. I went to the racetrack in Harrisburg because they were hiring cashiers. That's where I met a 6 foot, light skinned Cheshire cat (he had the biggest, prettiest, white teeth smile) who had the gift of charm and gab. We laughed, played around, and teased each other during the interview periods. The next thing I knew, I was a bit smitten, and I wrote my telephone number on the back of one of the betting tickets, fully intending to give it to him, which I did. Butch called the next day. We talked a bit, laughed some more, and he shared he was working as a bus driver. So cool, right?!

Butch said he would come by to see me later in the week. One afternoon, I heard beeping in front of the house. When I looked out the window, there was a big old yellow school bus parked with the door open. Guess who was sitting in the driver's seat with his hand holding the door lever wide open, grinning? I walked out to talk, and he said, "Get in." I asked, "What?" He said, "Get in." So, I got in. We went back to the bus depot where he parked the bus. Then we got into his car, and he drove me home.

We dated for about a year and were married in 1979. Butch became my first husband. I was still somewhat of a prude morally and sexually. It was important for me to be married in a church and before having children. Butch had been married before and had children from that marriage. He also had children with two other women in the city. He had a very colorful life previous to me. I had my standards and insisted on a church marriage. I needed him to come to church with me.

I believe in open communication, and I wanted him to keep a relationship with all his children. So, I needed to know about all previous relationships that he had children with, meet the children, and let their mothers know that their children were welcomed in my home. And, if they needed to speak with Butch about their children, it was fine, but they were not to engage in deception or play games with me or him.

Butch, as you can imagine, was charming and outgoing, and he liked to drink. So, he frequented bars often. I did go with him on occasion, but that became boring unless we could dance. We went to the local legion and had a good time dancing and laughing, meeting his family and friends.

We got pregnant, and I knew I wanted my child to have faith in God and a foundation that is beyond man. I was also looking for a state job. I met a lady while in the lobby of a state building and she was very warm and sweet. She asked me what I was doing. I shared that I wanted a state job, and Parks and Recreation jobs were in this building. I shared that I had a bachelor's degree in Recreation. I was also looking for a church home. She had a friend in HR and asked for my resume so she could send it to her. She also invited me to try her church, Goodwin Memorial Baptist Church (GMBC), which was right down the street. I agreed to visit the church one Sunday. She said she would look for me.

When I visited GMBC, I did not see the lady I met in the building lobby, but I loved the warmth of the church, I loved the worship, the sermon was moving, and they had a children's program. It was important that my children receive a religious background.

The choir was the bomb-diggity and moved my heart. When the pastor opened the doors of the church for baptism and membership, I popped up out of my seat. It scared me as my conscious mind began to doubt the action of my body. This was my first time at this church, and I was going down the aisle to receive Jesus and join the church. I was a little apprehensive of what others must think of me going down the aisle on my first visit to this church. Me and some others were ushered to the back room of the church; we were welcomed, and we gave our information and were told that a deacon would be in touch in a few days.

Not long after joining GMBC, I was hired in Pennsylvania State Parks and Recreation Department as a Recreation Specialist. I was overjoyed. I began working and, at lunchtime, I would look for the lady. I didn't see her at lunch for a couple of months; I figured she had left her job there. She was a secretary and already had several years with the state. As luck would have it, we finally met at lunch. She noticed I was pregnant, and she shared she had some health issues and had not been at work for a while. I informed her of all the wonderful things that had happened to me since our first meeting. I told her she was like an angel to me and thanked her for her kindness and all the help she provided. We became friends and for me, she, Anna, was a "spiritual mom."

Anna was so happy, and she helped me study the Bible and told me to read the book of John. I was obedient to study. It came upon me that I am not God. I will never know what God knows. I needed His supernatural power to work in my life, and I wanted Him in my child's life. I submitted to just believing and having faith and seeing what the end would be. I began my journey of having peace and not always having to be in control of things. I could relax and trust God.

In 1980, I gave birth to a son and we named him Dustin. One afternoon that same year, I was cooking in our kitchen with the back door open. It was a wonderful sunny day with a breeze coming in. The verse from John 3:16 was posted to the front of my refrigerator. There, I went into tears, crying and understanding how God loved me so much that He gave His only Son just for me, and I knew I loved my son and would die for him.

At that time, I think I fully grasped that I was loved and protected. It was not by anything I had done or could do. The breeze coming in was like a gentle, wonderful, peaceful, warmth that engulfed me. I was in it to win it. I was hungry for the word of God and wanted to develop my personal relationship with God, Jesus, and the Holy Spirit.

Being a good friend is a very good thing.
"Therefore encourage each other up,
just as in fact you are doing."
1 Thessalonians 5:15 NIV

From my perspective, I was not well-liked by Butch's family or siblings, probably because I was judgmental and their cursing, drinking and inappropriate movies that were playing while children were at the parties was unheard of, from my point of view, and unlike my family dynamic. His first wife, the mother of two of his children, was loud and had a more outgoing personality. She was invited to come to the family gatherings on the weekends, but I never made a scene at these events.

No one went to church. I was straight laced quiet. I did not like the favoritism that was an ongoing dynamic in this family and, after my two children were born, I put my foot down. I made the decision not to subject my children to the favoritism and adult atmosphere there and to not attend these family gatherings very often. I spoke to Butch about this change prior to and he was not happy, but he went along with the decision. (Regretfully, due to my decision early on, my children did not form lasting positive relations with their dad's side of the family.)

We got our own apartment. He was working off and on and I was taking care of the home and children. The plan was to eventually get a starter home and raise our family and their extended siblings. We were able to purchase a HUD home. We were active in church, and Butch was singing in the choir. Things were good for about a year.

Then, he had jobs on and off, he began to drink more and attend the local bars more. I became disillusioned about his ability to take care of us. He had promised things with our children would be different, even better, and he would not abandon us. But without a regular job, how could that happen? I became more selfish and put myself into the children and not so much into him. I am sure he could feel indifference from me.

Suppressed Anger and Explosion

As I matured, it appeared that my brother, Al, had more concern and care for his friends and less care for the privacy of their family, just like our father. My anger had been building up and was suppressed in me. It was about to come out.

One summer, my children stayed at Al's house in Johnstown. We were adamant that our children should know their cousins and have positive childhood experiences. His children enjoyed sports like baseball, football, and track, just like mine. I chose to stay overnight and return to Harrisburg the next day. My makeshift bedroom was their front room, where I slept on the couch.

Al stayed out late partying and came home with a buddy. The buddy was invited in and Al's partner, Kat, got up and began cooking breakfast for them. Well, this was eerily familiar, and I angrily went off on everyone like an 8-day alarm clock. It's their home, but it was my bedroom and there I sat in my robe, at the crack of dawn, while my privacy and sleep had been violated / invaded, and Al was happy to entertain the buddy with no regard for me. My brother looked shocked as this was coming from his little crybaby sister. The buddy apologized. At that moment, I chose to get dressed and take my kids and go home.

Later, during the 3-hour drive back to Harrisburg, I was able to reflect and acknowledge the total disrespect and anger I apparently felt as a child for me and my siblings. Our family was simultaneously and abruptly disrupted with the people-pleasing and on-demand performances we did as children. I no longer was going to accept this as an appropriate family dynamic. Someone in this sibling group needed to be a change agent and hopefully break the toxic cycle. I apparently was the one chosen. The repressed anger was justified and freeing as the tears ran down my cheeks. My kids remained quiet on the drive home. I was able to smooth things over with my brother and his family. Al said he remembered those times and understood.

Marital Betrayal

During my first marriage, I found out Butch was cheating on me at the local bar. Of course, he denied it and our relationship became more argumentative and accusing. Like a private eye, I followed him around to find out where his mistress lived. I confronted her at her home, and she came to our home threatening to fight. I had a baseball bat on the ready and my nosy neighbor, Ms. Hill, was looking out the window watching the drama unfold. (She is and has always been her own kind of gun-toting character.) This was the last straw for me. I decided we needed to break up and get a divorce and he could be with whoever he wanted. But I wanted to stay at home with the children.

He declared he wasn't going to leave so I called my sister who owned an apartment building. We moved into a one-bedroom apartment while, supposedly, Butch was making mortgage payments on the house. He never came around to visit the children. He never asked to take the children and spend time with them. He was working for the federal government at the military base, so I filed for support payments. I took a few drama-filled trips there to get him to pay for the house and help me take care of the kids, but to no avail.

He finally left our home and demanded that I give him the washer and dryer from the basement, as he had moved in with the mistress and I had moved back into our home with the kids. We fought over the washer and dryer for a couple of months, until I was in the basement- crying, angry, heartbroken, and trying to get clean clothes for the kids. I rationalized that I would not continue in this disarrayed emotional state. I decided, "It *ain't got nothing to do with the washer and dryer. Let him have the dang washer and dryer. I had a job and could buy another set.*" So, I left a message for him to come get the washer and dryer. He never came to get them.

But he did leave me with unpaid mortgages for several months. I had to be proactive and make special arrangements to protect my credit rating and keep our home. I had to get a "remodification" mortgage to slowly pay extra to keep the house. I was so freaking mad at him. How could he leave us, break his promise and live with another woman, her kids, and not take care of his own? I hated him for a long time. I listened to a lot of sermons from T.D. Jakes and music from John P. Kee to get through this emotional betrayal of a marriage.

I continued to work and salvage the mortgage on our home. Our neighborhood on Rolleston St. was good to us. We had a village within the neighborhood. We looked after each one's children. We communicated to various parents if we saw neighborhood kids doing something that was shady. The Boy's Club was around the corner across from the projects on the south side. The instructor there would inform the moms if our kids were acting out or hanging out with a not so good group of kids. He would address us as "Hey, Mom." They thought the diverse people on Rolleston St. were rich, but we also had our characters and neighborhood gossip.

All the kids played together and were invited to each other's birthday parties or sleep overs. Some of the parents would race in the streets with the kids, namely me. I would win a lot of the races. My son was the firecracker guy. He would buy firecrackers during the holidays for the neighborhood and set them off in the church parking lot to the amazement and excitement of everyone.

Our playground was just down the street, and we could hear parents calling the kids names or whistling the kids in for dinner or calling them to come home before the streetlights came on. I loved being part of this community, even with a broken heart and with the broken promises from Butch. I needed to **be bold and summon up my God-strength.**

"He heals the brokenhearted and binds up their wounds."
Psalm 147:3

"And we know that for those who know God,
all things work together for good for those who
are called according to His purpose."
Romans 8:28

Baby Danielle and Dustin, Rolleston Street

Young Verilyn with Dustin and Danielle

CHAPTER 12

Trailblazer

"You will break generational cycles and change. You have been anointed as a trailblazer, a cycle breaker, a miracle worker. You will be, according to some, peculiar, too sensitive, a misfit. Don't be misunderstood or considered too much by some. The truth is, you're enough, you're enough, you're more than enough. You will carry your name into a new dimension. Eyes have not seen, ears have not heard nor have entered the imagination, what you should be. So, when you walk into the room and you're the only one that looks like you, fear not. You are there on assignment, to shift the atmosphere. You might be the first, but you won't be the last. Hold the door open, pull the door open. Sitting in the land looks strange, look again even in the new environment, there is a great cloud of witnesses praying for you. Your great grandmothers are in the room praying for you. Don't you dare

put your head down. Head up, shoulders back! Head up, shoulders back! They have not done you a favor, you belong there. Your community is with you. God is with you, and you will not fail, and you will not fail. You must be willing to go into a city, a department, a position that no one before you have ever done before." ~ Dr. Thema Bryant

The above sermon by Dr. Bryant resonated with me. I believe God has always been on my side, and my guardian angel continues to oversee the divine charge, however small, on my life.

God is faithful! He keeps his promises.

One of the many state applications I submitted was for a job working inside the State Correctional Institution at Camp Hill (SCIC). I was contacted and invited in for an interview for the position of Pennsylvania State Activities Specialist.

I was excited and a bit apprehensive about working in a state prison. I knew very little about prison. Once again, I thought it was just an interview, and I met the qualifications. They would be assessing me, and I would be assessing them for a good fit. **I needed to be bold and summon up my God-strength, for God is with me.** I can do all things with God on my side.

Upon being interviewed, I answered questions as educated and as confidently as I could without having the experience or knowledge of what goes on in a prison, barring what I had seen on TV.

One of my mottos is, "What's for me is for me."

Let the chips fall where they may.
Follow my example, as I follow the example of Christ.
"Take a risk. Dare to be unique in Jesus."
1 Corinthians 11:1 NIV

I was hired for the position. Then I got nervous and called everyone. I revered their opinion of me and wanted them to give me honest feedback and to encourage my ability to do the job. I called Mom, my sister, and received that confident, bolstering encouragement. I gave a silent prayer of thanks to the mighty God who continues to make a way and opens doors for me.

"So do not fear, for I am with you; do not be dismayed,
for I am your God. I will strengthen you and help you;
I will uphold you with my righteous right hand."
Isaiah 41:10

God is present with me in every situation and what is for me is for me. He will never abandon me. I went into the interview with much more confidence and had mentally chosen to do the best I could do, and the outcome would be up to God. Thank God. I could earn more money to take care of my kids.

I didn't know a whole lot about prison, but I figured I was an Affirmative Action double dipper, meaning I was a woman and Black who presented with experience, Chutzpah, some positive ethics, integrity, and character.

In March 1984, I began my training and received a tour of the facilities. I met the other employees and inmates who would acclimatize me to the culture, rules and parts of the physical education program I would be responsible for. I was looking them over and they were sizing me up.

I was the **first woman and Black woman** to work as an Activities Specialist at a male prison in the state of

Pennsylvania. Look at God! My job was to work deep inside the prison, directly with the male population, in a gym at the far south end of the prison. I had to be bold, look and act fearless, and never let them see me sweat.

From the gym, the route to get to other parts of the SCIC prison was a long walk between the set of inmate housing units called the H-J-K blocks which were situated on the right side of the walkway. The education building, which housed the library, was on the left. As I continued to walk, the chapel located on the right. Looking straight ahead was the office building and the roll call room for officers upon starting and leaving their shift. I needed to make a left-hand turn at the intersection to get to the cafeteria for lunch and then return to the gym the same way and finish my workday.

I have had various experiences walking that path over the years. I was put on notice from other male staff that they didn't believe a woman should be working in population and without a male escort, on top of that! How dare me! They said the administration was out of their fxxxking minds. The officers believed that protecting the woman increased the danger of their jobs, making it unfeasible.

I started work at SCIC, determined to do a fantastic job and to keep my wits about me, knowing I had something to prove. I could do this job, and I would make me, my family, and women proud. I was a change agent, a trailblazer, a cycle breaker. God placed me in a position that no other woman had been in before. I was enough! But was it always easy? Heck no.

I was also willing to learn. During the first days to weeks, I was in observation mode. The office inmates who worked at the gym were helpful in explaining what they do, where, and how to make callout lists. I saw how they greeted and allowed the incoming inmates to get that personal look at the woman who worked in the gym.

Unbeknownst to me, the Black boxing coach told his boxers to watch out for me while at the prison. The coach knew it would be a difficult position as the first woman and first Black woman to work in a medium level male prison. I found this out from an inmate years after the boxing coach retired. I was grateful and honored that this man who didn't know my character or my motives had seen the need to cover me just on the basis of me being a woman and Black. Again, look at God!

CHAPTER 13

New Dimension

My first day consisted of getting the keys to the gym and initiating and establishing relationships with office inmate staff, my supervisor Kirk K. and my colleague Terry B., who gave me a tour of the gym area.

I had an assigned desk near the picture window where I could observe the inmates participating in various indoor sports. There was one restroom, and Terry had made it into a co-ed restroom, meaning he had cleaned it. When I needed to use it, he advised me to put a sign on the door and lock it. In his dry humor manner, he seemed pretty proud of his attempt to make me comfortable. He shared what sports I would take over for the inmates, and he announced to the inmate staff that there would be no more loitering and hanging out in the gym office unless they were doing required work, like typing and such.

Terry, always the straight shooter, let me know from the jump street that he was not for women working directly in population with the inmates. He felt he needed to protect me, and it made more work for him and added to his responsibility. I also am a straight shooter, and I responded to him this way. *"Rest easy. I can take care of myself and will not be an added burden to you. I just need to learn how things operate, and I will make the necessary adjustments to do the job."*

I certainly was a big curiosity. There were many inmates who had signed up to be in the sports program to get a good personal look at the woman in the gym. My attire consisted of wearing coordinated sweat suits and my adidas game was on point. I purposely sat on the bleachers in the gym so all could have a good look. I observed the men (inmates) wearing mostly boxer shorts and their junk was flipping and flopping all over the place. On occasions during the basketball game, a penis would show its naked face. The inmate would hurriedly put his junk back into the boxer short opening. Also, high vigilance was given to my reaction when this occurred. I was cool and remained non-reactive. It wasn't the first time I had seen a penis.

Later, I shared the changes I would immediately implement in the gym. It was announced that effective the next day, to participate in the sports in and outside the gym, all men needed to sew up the openings in their boxer shorts and / or preferably wear shorts of some kind to the gym.

They needed to have a pass to get into and participate in the gym. This was another opportunity for the inmates to get a closer look as I received their pass. I got various attitudinal responses as well as verbal comments. They were adjusting to me and my no-nonsense personality. I learned that I needed to be strict from the beginning and could let up later once I had established and earned the respect of the inmates. I could have fun and have a kind attitude if that's how they approached me. I could also handle their disrespect, if I needed to.

As time elapsed, some tried to tell me how to dress or wear or not wear makeup. I reminded them of a mother, sister, or girlfriend. I did receive love letters as they tried me throughout my career at SCIC. I would return the letters to them on a one-to-one basis. I attempted to respect them in being firm and giving them a hard NO. Their charm and flattery did not impress me, explaining that I was not there for romance and / or relationship shenanigans. I wasn't trying to get a man. I had no motive except to get paid and take care of my family.

There were many times the male officers who needed to come in and monitor the showers in the evenings would attempt to throw their weight around by giving orders to the inmates not in the showers. I stood in my power and let them know this was my area and all they needed to do was go to the showers to get the inmates showered and I had the other part.

Of course, the scuttlebutt was on high inside the prison and news traveled fast that I was working at the gym. That is where I met Sgt. Reily. She was a stout woman, and she loved her cigarettes. She would make her rounds, and we often chatted about the ordeals she had as the first female officer who came from a female prison to SCIC. Over the years, she gave me valuable advice and camaraderie. There was another (2nd) female officer, Ms. Kennedy, who worked on various blocks. I did not get a chance to meet her. I would also be called to the main entrance or visitors area to search female visitors and or supervise visitors. I was given advice not to date the correctional officers because all they were looking for was a notch on their belt.

I grew and matured while working in the prison, as God gave me many opportunities to reflect on how to handle different situations. When walking to and from the gym, there were many times I was yelled at and called "bitch" or some other vulgarity. (I was called everything except a child of God.) I tried to get the inmates and officers to investigate and or share if they heard someone bragging about the verbal vulgarities hurled at me. There were times I yelled back, *"If you want to speak with me, come on down to the gym. Be a man; let's do it face to face."*

"You are my hiding place; you shall preserve me from trouble; you shall surround me with songs of deliverance. Selah"
Psalm 32:7 NKJV

But that's not to say that the name calling did not impact me. **Again, I needed to summon my God-strength and insert what God thinks of me and who God says I am and whose I am.** I needed to reflect on my socialization of the word "bitch." I knew the meaning of it as it referred to a female dog. I knew the degrading name it was meant for a woman, and it was a fighting word in the hood. I reframed that word, and it ceased to affect me negatively.

After a while, I ignored the ignorance of those inmates. Eventually it stopped. I didn't know the reason, whether the inmates were transferred to another prison or block or got tired because I was no longer reactive to their words.

There were times while in the main yard when approximately 200 plus inmates were in close proximity to me and one would try to cop a feel on my butt. It happened the first time. I reported it, to no avail, as I didn't know who it was. So, I learned to walk around the yard with my hands loosely clasped behind me. I was able to chase down an inmate the second time it occurred, and he got the consequence, even with his denial of the action.

Some inmates thought of me as their imaginary girlfriend, of which I shared, "That's not my kinda party." It was hard for some inmates to understand I really did not want them. I taught recreational life skill classes and helped the lifers sell ice cream.

From the late 1980s to 1990s when HIV/Aids swept across the United States, many men were being incarcerated as well. The men called it the "hot shit." I worked with the inmates who were isolated and placed by the hospital. I was assigned to bring board games for them to have some type of recreation periods. They were appreciative to see me and to be able to talk to someone, as they were very much feared by other inmates. They might as well have scarlet letters on their foreheads. No staff or other inmates wanted to be near them. They had their own of everything. Everyone was adamant about using their PPEs (personal protection equipment) during these years until the stigma was minimized and the fear factor of catching HIV/Aids de-escalated. (My main fear working in the prison was of walking up on two males having a homosexual affair, but that never happened.)

During the first two years working at the prison, I was going through a divorce. There were times I cried before going to work, yet I had to get it together emotionally to deal with my job. There were two or three lifers who, for the life of me, always came to the gym with the biggest and brightest smiles. They appeared to be happy and full of fun. They gave me joy (Kyle was one) and my thought on this was, *"If they can have joy as they are doing life in prison daily, what in the world am I moping around about?"* I was sad and angry about my poor choice of a father for my children and his abandonment / betrayal of our family.

I was sitting in the library one evening on prison campus and I read a poster on the wall. It helped to snap me out of the emotional bag I was in:

"Tis better to have loved and lost than
to never have loved at all."
~ Alfred Lord Tennyson

It seems to have encapsulated the bittersweetness of my life at that time. I was promised one thing and received another. Love is a risk. Love can enrich our lives and add a meaningful layer of experience that I would not have known if I hadn't taken the risk. So, I needed to detach and move on with my life. I had other goals to achieve. One unsuccessful marriage would not stop my progress. I had to suck it up, buttercup!

> Yes, you are on purpose! You are right
> where God wants you to be.
> *"God has great plans for you, says the Lord.*
> *They are for your good....to give you a future and a hope."*
> *Jeremiah 29:11 NLT*

An email from Terence "Terry" B. dated January 24, 2025

> *For my friend Verilyn Jackson-Downing (Joy for my Journey). I appreciate your love and respect for my part of your work life as the first female to be hired in a male correctional institution as a corrections activities specialist.*
>
> *Correctional activities specialist job responsibilities were mainly athletics, music, art, inmate organizations, etc. The following are memories I have of our years together as colleagues.*
>
> *I started my career in Corrections in September 1976. Within 6 months, my supervisor retired, and I was by myself. I made a lot of mistakes and earned my master's degree in corrections the hard way.*
>
> *When a new supervisor was hired, he told me he interviewed candidates for an open position in our department and hired a woman (VJD).*

I was totally against this decision and expressed my opinion! I believed the inmates would want to impress her and I would have to break up more fights and put additional pressure on myself to keep her safe. I also did not like the idea that I would have to supervise all the showering at the end of the activity.

I admit I was totally wrong. The inmates became lover boys and the atmosphere in the gym calmed down. VJD told me she received numerous love letters from inmates, which I understand.

The inmates played basketball, etc., in their boxer shorts, which exposed their genitals. Her response to me was, "Nothing I haven't seen before." However, for the sake of decency, all men would need to wear shorts over their underwear. I was not impressed with the inmates Johnsons swinging back and forth and out of their boxers.

A boxing match was conducted on the main recreation field with over 1,000 inmates present. VJD and I were assigned to supervise this event along with a handful of corrections officers. I remember walking 10 feet behind her through the crowd of inmates and someone grabbed her ass. VJD turned around and was about to earn back her respect, but we both could not identify who the culprit was. I am sure that the inmate enjoyed himself that night in his cell.

We played tackle football at the prison just like the movie, The Longest Yard. It was between the inmate housing units and not the guards. I was the referee and VJD was the line judge in her very first game. A play finished in front of her, and she did not have a clue about forward progress to spot the ball. We both had smiles on our faces after the play. Pretty similar to football officials today.

I also remember when VJD went to use the bathroom in our staff dressing room. This room was an open space concept which meant no doors or curtains. The window in this room had individual frosted panes except for 3 clear replacement panes. I found inmates crawling over each other to look through these 3 clear windowpanes. We found a portable screen to offer her some privacy.

In 1985 when I was promoted to Activities Manager, I asked VJD to replace me as the coach of the varsity basketball team. Our schedule included other correctional institutions and college JV basketball teams. She accepted the challenge, knowing only the basic rules about the sport, but with her learning spirit, she was always ready to improve her skills from anyone willing to teach her. We worked together to continue to make it a successful program for the inmates.

Through my experience working with VJD, out of a staff of 8 employees, 3 were women working at the same time in the activities department.

My hope is that Verilyn Jackson-Downing and I will remain friends for life.

Terry B.

CHAPTER 14

A Better Me

I continued to grow and mature, always wanting to earn my master's degree. I would often have time while supervising the sports games and events to share and give counsel to many of the inmates. As time went on, many encouraged me and would often state I should be a counselor. I would thank them but not seriously consider it. But I had planned to go back to college when my children entered high school and were more independent.

There was this unspoken rule among the Blacks. We always tried to make sure we spoke to and got to know each other as there were not that many Blacks working at the prison. However, it appears I missed keeping that rule on one occasion.

Two new officers, Arthur and a friend, had just been hired and were coming in at the main gate when I was exiting to go to the personnel office. According to Arthur, I had my head up and ignored them. Arthur wanted to speak to / greet me, so he inquired about me with the main gate officers.

I would see Officer Arthur mainly in the late evening in the cafeteria as he worked the second shift. I was watching him from time to time and had concluded that he was into himself and arrogant. I also would eat late meals with the officer who worked in the educational building. Officer Freddie would call Officer Arthur over to eat with us. We had great conversations as I was opinionated, curious, and liked to get into people's heads to see where they were coming from. Officer Arthur was well-spoken, had a good sense of humor, and seemed to have some intelligence about himself. So, he became tolerable during our random late meals at work.

Of course, I didn't date anyone at the prison for a long time. Eventually Officer Arthur suggested going out on a date, but I refused the offer. Then Officer Freddie suggested we double date one weekend. I was open to that. Our random meet ups in the cafeteria became more frequent and I gave him my number. We went on our first date to a bar uptown, which was then a club. Officer Arthur was very charming with a gift of gab, and he presented as caring and having good manners. He didn't mind spending money during the dates either. So, I was impressed, to the point we had our first sexual encounter on our first date night.

Arthur lived a distance from the prison. We began to date and had an on-and-off relationship. When it was good it was good, and when it was bad, it was bad. I always had questions about his relationship with the mother of his child. He was not one to openly share what was going on in his life, so there were lingering questions and suspicions.

The prison soon saw us as a couple. We dated about one and a half years. He didn't meet my children until I felt like the relationship was getting serious. Eventually, Officer Arthur proposed to me while he was drunk. I refused this proposal and told him he would need to propose to me when he was sober and knew exactly what he was saying and doing. He did. I accepted. I wanted to be married in the church and the pastor believed that because my first husband was still alive, we needed to get his permission to get married so not to be in adultery. I made sure he was divorced from his first wife and had some conversations with his child and my children.

As the dating/courtship went, so did the marriage. When it was good, it was good, and when it was bad, it was bad. There was competition in our marriage, infidelity, domestic violence, marriage counseling, separation, and getting back together.

Carol's Medical Needs

During this time, Carol, my sister, endured her body turning on itself until she needed to get kidney dialysis weekly. She continued dialysis until her doctors said she needed a kidney transplant. She called and asked me to come to her home. Hesitantly she asked if I would be willing to get tested to find out if my kidney could be a match for her. Without hesitation, it was a resounding yes. I watched her shoulders drop with a sigh of relief. My sister was a Jehovah's Witness and that meant she could not get a blood transfusion. With me as donor, she would not need to.

We each had to donate blood to be used during surgery, if needed. In 1988, I donated my left kidney to my wonderful sister. She was able to live, dialysis-free, for about 10 years before issues began arising due to other organs deteriorating. We enjoyed many joyful years and laughter prior to her untimely transition in 1998 at the age of 48.[10]

It was great to have SCIC benefits during this time because I was able to take time off to heal from the surgery to remove my kidney. Then, after what seemed like a long time away, I returned to work ready for another change.

SCIC Drug and Alcohol Program

SCIC had a contained (inpatient) Drug and Alcohol program for the inmates. I got to know the Administrator (Marshal) of the program. We would eat lunch together, and I would pick his brain about drug and alcohol addiction issues. Remember, I came from a family where I came to believe my father was a functional alcoholic.

I also loved the psychology of humans. I became more and more interested in looking into the career of counseling or being a social worker. I was beginning to believe that I did have a talent/gift for working with people and wanted to help them help themselves. I asked to be considered for an open position in the drug program.

I began training in the inpatient drug program as a Drug and Alcohol Specialist. It was an interesting transition. I shadowed a co-worker and began to read about addiction and experience the group work and individual counseling skills.

Below is an email I received from a friend, Bernie C., on November 6, 2024.

> *When I started working for the Department of Corrections in 1989, corrections was predominantly a male-oriented field. When staff were hired, they were designated as either contact staff or non-contact staff, depending on the interaction they had with inmates. Although female staff were*

employed, the majority of them worked in non-contact clerical positions. When institutional issues would arise, non-contact female clerical staff would be escorted to a secure area out of harm's way.

The few females that were designated as contact staff were primarily medical or treatment staff (counselors, psychologists, or drug and alcohol). Female staff represented a relatively small percentage of the overall institutional complement. When hired as a Drug and Alcohol Treatment Specialist, I was assigned to the institution's therapeutic community. The therapeutic community was an intensive, long-term program, and the only one of its kind in the state system. The program was limited to 40 inmates, chosen from institutions across the state and staffed by very competent supervisor (Mr. Kressler) and two primary treatment specialists.

It was there that I had my first interaction working with female staff inside a male institution. Ms. Downing had initially started her career as an activity specialist but transferred over to the drug and alcohol department as a treatment specialist. We facilitated groups and treatment activities both together and separately within the therapeutic community. Although I had been involved in providing drug and alcohol treatment in the community for several years prior to accepting my position at corrections, my experience working with incarcerated males was limited to facilitating a few groups a week at a county prison.

As one might expect, dealing with this population on a full-time basis presented some unique challenges. Initially, I was a "sponge" trying to absorb as much information as possible for more seasoned, experienced staff. Fortunately, I was blessed with the coworkers and supervisors who were willing to provide guidance and mentorship.

I learned a great deal from co-facilitating groups with Miss Downing, including the importance of structure, consistency, boundaries, and identifying manipulation with this population. Working with a female in this male dominated environment was unique, to say the least. I noticed how inmates, and sometimes staff, would treat females differently. Sometimes they did not take them as seriously as their male counterpart or perceived that they were more easily manipulated.

I watched as inmates would frequently attempt to test the limits with female staff. Although working in a prison is challenging for any staff person, I realized it was much more of a challenge for female staff. This experience changed my perspective and resulted in a newfound respect for any female staff who could successfully navigate a correctional career.

When I was promoted to a supervisory position in the Drug and Alcohol department, about half of my staff were females. It was during this period that I started to realize the advantages of diversity and viewing situations from different perspectives. Having this unique blend of staff increased dialogue when attempting to resolve inmate or departmental issues and allowed us to explore solutions "outside the box." That may not have been an option with an all-male staff.

I believe this actually made me more objective, and a better supervisor over my 35-year career in corrections. I have worked for, worked with, and supervised a number of female staff and, undoubtedly, became better for those interactions. Over the years, more and more females entered the correctional field. As the number of females increased, so did the opportunity for advancement. Time and time again, females proved their value and competency (although this was no easy task). They started to move into management positions and, eventually, into elite levels of leadership. We now have several female institutional superintendents and a female Secretary of Corrections. Corrections have come a long way over the past 30 to 40 years and we are indebted to those early Trail Blazers like Ms. Downing.

Bernie C.

CHAPTER 15

Riotous Living

"Be strong and courageous. Do not be afraid or terrified because of them, for the Lord your God goes with you; he will never leave you nor forsake you."
Deuteronomy 31:6-8

"It is not the things we get, but the hearts we touch that will measure our success in life." Charlie Brown

"Just because I can't sing, doesn't mean I won't sing." Elizabeth Majeed

I was off duty when the prison riot occurred and received the news from the TV. Of course, we are considered essential employees, and it was chaotic trying to get information as to whether I should get to work or wait. Let me share some historical facts about this nationwide event.

At 2:45 PM on Wednesday, October 25th, 1989, at the state correctional institution at Camp Hill, a suburb of Harrisburg, the state capital, an inmate punched a guard during a routine move while bringing inmates inside after yard time. When an undetermined number of prisoners assaulted a staff employee in gatehouse E, at least one guard was taken hostage, and there could be more.

Efforts were being made to begin negotiations with the prisoners. About 70 state troopers in riot gear and a surveillance helicopter were sent to the prison compound. At least 25 fire companies and about 15 ambulances were also sent.

Inmates occupied part of the state's largest prison. On Wednesday, they took at least one guard hostage and set two fires, the condition of the hostages had not been determined. Six of the 10 cell blocks were gutted so severely that it was a year before the last block was restored for occupation. The buildings were vandalized, burned to the ground, and suffered extensive smoke damage. Three days of rioting happened at Camp Hill prison. By the time the riots ended, 138 corrections officers had been injured. 70 inmates set fires and went on a vandalism spree destroying 14 of the prisons' 31 buildings. Overcrowding was a factor, as a prison housed more than double the number of inmates for which it was designed. After the riots, the state spent millions of dollars repairing and improving the prison.

Each employee and inmate who was present at Camp Hill prison during the 1989 riots now knows that a seemingly safe and predictable world can collapse at any time without warning. Even staff who were off duty when the riots occurred become anxious when they think about what might have happened to them, if they had been on duty at the time of the riot. Many staff members accept the uncertainty of their jobs and show no outward sign of the anxiety they harbor within. Other staff accept the uncertainty of prison life and function normally because of the resources of their religion, background or emotional capabilities. Some staff cannot face the possibility of another riot and leave corrections. Adversity, however, can make the correctional staff as a whole stronger and wiser.

I knew that rebuilding trust and care between inmates and correctional staff was a long row to hoe. The men and women came together in a camaraderie that was embraced by all. With the prison locked down for months, all staff on their 10-hour shifts would come to the cafeteria and get food and the trays for the inmates to be fed. Some officers slept at the prison because some of the men and women travelled from the coal regions to work at Camp Hill. Many worked lots of overtime. We all worked like clockwork. We maintained our professionality and completed the tasks assigned.

We were all acutely aware of those who were taken hostage, injured and were otherwise destructively coping with the aftermath. Slowly the inmates were sorted/determined who could be confined in a less restrictive manner. Some of those inmates were the inmates I worked with who were part of the therapeutic (inpatient) Drug and Alcohol patients. Group work was phased in so they could be debriefed. This may sound crazy, but it was the worst of times and the best of times simultaneously.

Fear did not affect me except for one time when I sensed a spirit of evil lingering near a group of men who were returning from spiritual activities, which made me shudder.

My Continued Growth

Between 1995 and 2000, I set my mind to accomplish my personal goal of going to graduate school. The undergraduate degree had been for my parents; the master's degree was for me!

I matriculated into Shippensburg University for my graduate degree in Community Counseling. I was still working in the drug and alcohol field. However, the prison had gone through a transition and became a classification prison. The therapeutic community, or inpatient drug and alcohol program, was terminated at SCIC. Correctional Drug and Alcohol counselors moved above the gymnasium where inmates were being tested psychologically, and drug and alcohol assessments were completed.

I also had a part-time counseling position with Daikon Lutheran Social Services in Mechanicsburg, Pa. I was able to use both the corrections drug and alcohol program and counseling foster children at Daikon as part of my internships for my graduate degree.

While doing all these things, out of the clear blue, the Mother from my church verbalized that I would be working with children. I was a bit stunned, yet I just politely asked, "Really?" Upon walking away, I thought to myself, "She is crazy. I like working with adults. They can generally reason things out." What will be will be. I thanked her and moved on.

I had the best supervisors and co-workers while working in corrections. Life was hectic, good, exhausting, stimulating, yet all my goals were coming together. Looking back, it was a blur. I promised to be a sloth when I retired. **God's strength again kept me.**

I have always loved working for direct services. I graduated from Shippensburg University in 2000. I was able to obtain counseling licenses such as (LPC) Licensed Professional Counselor in Pa., (NCC) National Certified Counselor, and licensure in drug and alcohol. I have been in several other positions at SCIC such as Drug and Alcohol Program Analyst and the latter 5 years I paroled myself to be Corrections Counselor in two Community Corrections Centers (York and Harrisburg).

CHAPTER 16

Changes

The Attack of 9-11

I decided that I would parole myself from inside the prison and get work at the halfway house. My first position outside of the state corrections prison walls was going to the halfway house in York, Pa. I worked there for a couple of years waiting to get into the Harrisburg halfway house as a correctional counselor. My time at the York halfway house was the same year as the September 11, 2001 attacks. These were a series of airline hijackings and suicide attacks committed by 19 terrorists associated with the Islamic extremist group Al-Qaeda. It was the deadliest terrorist attack on the USA soil; nearly 3,000 people were killed. The twin towers were taken down by hijacked airplanes in New York City.

I was working in my office at the halfway house and doing individual counseling appointments. One client shared with me that the world was ending. I asked, "What is going on?" He asked, "Haven't you heard that America's been attacked?"

When I looked at the TV, there were the two towers smoking and collapsing to the ground. Another plane was on its way to Washington, DC but was down in Pennsylvania. America was in shock and fear during this time.

This was an unbelievable, historical, traumatizing time in America. Panic and fear spread across the USA. No one knew exactly what to do immediately after the attacks. I called my family. I called my husband. I wanted to know the location of the children, their activities, and their emotional state. I was wondering if I should go home to be with them and make sure they were safe. They were OK. So, I decided to stay at work until the end of the day.

My Paradise

Arthur regularly attended church with me. We traveled together and took beautiful pictures of us, which were hanging in the hallways of our house. We entertained at home, bought a convertible BMW, and enjoyed life. Both of my husband's knew I planned to go to Arizona upon my retirement. I verbalized this often during our courtships. It is hard to concretely decipher how I came upon this notion. I remember seeing palm trees, a beautiful sunset and desert in a picture book and thought, "There is my paradise."

Arthur and I took trips to Arizona and found out they were building single dwellings – one floor, 3 bedrooms, two baths, and two car garages for less than 100k. This seemed fantastic and out of this world. I've always wanted to be a landowner, and I wanted to get my 40 acres and a mule that was promised to Black folks as reparations from slavery. (My car was my mule.) And I love the movie, "Gone with the Wind," because the thought of the main character was that you can always count on land.

I was nearing the time of retiring from state corrections. We discussed how we might do that so we could continue the prosperous life that we had built for ourselves.

Arizona was selling 40 acre ranches for a reasonable price under 50k. The thought was that we would have two homes if we could build a home in Arizona on the 40 acres and keep the home in Pennsylvania as a seasonal home. We could be snowbirds. He began to balk at those suggestions, so I took it upon myself to research homes and property information. He would hesitate and non-verbally tag along, not really committing to any of the long-term goals, so I moved forward on my own. I initiated the purchase of our 40 acre land.

But as we experienced changes in our marriage, the relationship was characterized by both respect and remorse. At one point during my second marriage, my husband hit me, broke my eardrums, and I needed surgery. After I called the police on him, my friend, Rosa, my second spiritual mom, mentor, and confidant, drove me to the doctor's office. She saved my life. She knew how to drive, yet she didn't drive. She chose to take a chance and drive without a driver's license to get me to the hospital. I was embarrassed and humiliated that I found myself in a domestic violence situation with someone who said they loved me. Arthur was ordered out of our home, but even then, I wanted to protect him from Rosa's judgment.

I was traumatized in every sense of the word. I was emotionally and verbally stunned, humiliated, hurt, sad, and never-ever thought I would be or would allow someone to hit me. As a child, I had observed an instance of domestic violence involving my parents and I resolved that I would not tolerate such behavior from my spouse, and if he ever tried, I would not stay with him. Now, here I was, faced with this violence. How could God allow this to happen to me? How could I be in a marriage where this happened? I was in a fog and couldn't put the pieces together.

As a counselor, I recognized the importance of addressing my own emotions and subsequently joined a support group at the YWCA in Harrisburg. It was difficult to utter the words, "victim of domestic violence" in the group. I was no longer a facilitator; I was a victim, and I needed to be a survivor. I needed to beat this. I learned, even more so, that facing the truth of the situation (no stinkin' thinkin'), being brutally honest, incorporated my own cognitive behavioral skills and were tantamount to my winning. In the counseling profession, it is considered important to guide individuals based on one's own experiences, education, wisdom, empathy, and acquired skills. Now I was having to turn those inward to help myself.

Arthur stayed away for 2-1/2 years and had counseling and attended anger management groups. Eventually we got back together with remorse and his promise that he would never hit me again. We began to focus on moving into a single detached home and purchased our home around late 2001. There was happiness with a dose of caution for me, but I didn't want another failed marriage. Things with us were seemingly good until I retired four years later.

I slowly began to suspect that things were not wonderful in my marriage. My husband was habitually going out on Thursday nights, spending not only his money but also the household money. He would stay out late into the late evening / early morning. I watched this behavior trend for a while and decided not to be excessively suspicious. I would not confront him immediately. I knew exactly what was happening because I found letters that were sent to my home from another woman he had been seeing.

I decided to investigate for myself. On two occasions, I followed him and my suspicions were verified; he was committing adultery. I knocked on the door of the woman where he parked the BMW. She came to the door, of course, and I asked for my husband. She let him know his wife was at the door, and he came out. I had words for her, as well, and of course her response was, "Well, what do I have to do with this?" My husband went into denial mode, which is common behavior when folks are caught red-handed. First they deny, then they blame, then they minimize their actions. He tried to make me think that I was not supposed to believe what I had seen with my own eyes. The infidelity had been going on for some months, which ended up being much longer than I suspected.

Here's what I did. I told myself, *"Stay strong and stick to the precise topic at hand. Do not allow him to gaslight you. You have learned the truth, Verily. The truth you have seen with your own eyes."* At some point, just like Tina Turner sang, I wondered, *what's love got to do with it?* I realized that a heart can be broken, and marriage needs more than love.

Arthur was a user of alcohol and a drug user of cocaine. He had anger and abandonment issues. We worked hard to purchase our home and to furnish it. Yet I was played. We had always been a throuple (a couple of three), plus. Arthur had a military buddy that he visited every Thursday night. He was so enmeshed in our marriage that it seemed like they had some type of homosexual relations.

Arthur got the women on the side and started being argumentative. He was a habitual person, although he thought he was slick. Give a person enough rope and he will hang himself. I chose not to deal with rumors. I caught him in the act of being unfaithful and he still tried to deny it. We entertained our friends in our home, and he made it a hoes den. I was hurt again. I knew at this point that I was pretty much done with the marriage. I was no longer invested.

The marital situation at home was tense and we were just marking time together. He tried to argue about every little thing even if he was in the wrong, and I would not take the bait to argue. He was not coming home at a decent hour as a married man; he wanted to argue about me not opening the door for him, but he could come through the garage to get in.

I began sleeping in the second bedroom. We began to basically live separate lives in our home. We spoke as was needed to pay bills and that was pretty much it. I did a lot of praying, crying, and having a pity party. I couldn't believe that my picker was off again, and that I had chosen another man who was not honoring the sanctity of marriage and didn't respect the marriage, or me and the life we had.

Again, facing the reality of the situation, I shared that I would like to move to Arizona and asked him if he would be coming along. There was never any verbal or behavioral commitment to do that. It was always, "I don't know. I'll think about it." To me, that was his way of saying no without committing to move to Arizona.

By this time, my son was in the military, and my daughter was off to college. I knew I could make these moves without a lot of uprooting of their lives. Of course, they were made aware of our broken relationship and marriage. They just wanted me to be happy, and they understood the situation.

I researched Arizona and looked at the areas where I might want to reside. I started connecting with my career what I would do after I got there. I wanted to work with the Native Americans doing either counseling or teaching. I researched the facilities there. I got my AZ identification to begin work with children and or the behavioral health field. I looked up apartment complexes where I might stay. I started to get my vehicle ready for travel. My intention was to drive there; I was still waiting for signs.

I planned to see if my husband would change his mind to move with me and make it a situation where we would become snowbirds, but again, he was non-committal to that idea. At this time, I was working at Harrisburg halfway house, looking to God and praying for guidance in the timing. I needed a divine sign to let me know it was time to go. After working in Harrisburg halfway and retiring in 2005, I began completing projects at our house that were put off until I had time to do them. And by this time, my husband was staying out all night. We were each living a single life in the same home.

Meanwhile, I began having contact/counseling relationships with young and older adults, trying to help them see themselves and make corrections to be better people. Things were coming together, but I was waiting for God to show me His direction. **God-strength again kept me.**

On a weekend in 2007, I was laying on the couch when he came home after drinking. He tried to argue and fight, even to the point of one more hit, one more act of violence. I reminded him, *"You said you would not hit me again."* He walked away.

On this day, I was in the kitchen concocting various ways I could make him feel some of the pain he had put me through in the marriage. Then the Lord said to my spirit, *"Be kind."* I answered, *"What? Be kind? Apparently, you don't know how much this man has hurt me!"*

I heard it again. *"Be kind."* I was obedient to the Holy Spirit. At times, it was difficult to muster up civility... kindness. **So, I know it was God's strength, not mine.**

> *"I am the vine, ye are the branches. He that abideth in me, and I in him, the same bringeth forth much fruit; for without me ye can do nothing.*

*I needed to depend on God to find real **strength** and **security**. I can't depend on man for man will disappoint. I must depend on God's sovereignty and his power. God is the only one who can meet my need of comfort, **strength**, peace, never leaving me alone. I want to be like the **tree** that stands by the river. God knows I am weak, and he is strong."*
John 15:5 KJV

"We are to not be anxious about anything but to instead pray and trust God with everything."
Philippians 16:13 KJV

At this point my husband said to me, "I do want a divorce, and you can file for the divorce." That was a pretty clear sign that I was on my own. The marriage had definitely deteriorated and was irreconcilable. I was agonizing over the move while curtailing my tongue and praying through domestic violence and second divorce.

One day, after shopping, I parked outside our home, not wanting to go inside. I had already ordered and installed the hitch on my vehicle but still hadn't decided when to leave. My Saturn and I just needed a date to get it done.

Rosa, My Second Spiritual Mom

CHAPTER 17

Move!

In 2007, while listening to gospel music, I heard a radio commercial about a prophetess visiting Harrisburg. Some of these small storefront churches brought in anointed folks to speak.

I needed to get a word from God, so I decided that I would find the storefront church and ease my spirit, ease my soul, and hopefully get a word that would be my sign to be a pioneer to Arizona. Once I got to the storefront church and I walked in, there were approximately 10 people in the church, including me, the pastor, and his wife. The pastor excitedly welcomed the folks in the congregation and spoke very highly of the woman of God, the prophetess, who had come to give a word.

I expected to get peace and a word about a decision I had made but was waiting on the timing. The Prophetess recorded her messages for different people without charging them. After speaking to several folks, she pointed to me and said, "The lady in the yellow-brown scarf, come up. I have a word for you." Surprised, I looked around to see who she was talking to. She said, "No. You. I want you to come up. I have a word for you." I went to the front of the church and raised my hands and worshiped. She said, "The Lord is asking me to ask you, 'Jonah, when are you gonna go?'" I crumbled in tears. That was my word and that was my sign. It was my time. I crumbled and cried. She whispered in my ear, "When you get there, the Lord says you will be prosperous; there will be wonderful blessings for you." Still crying, I walked back to my seat. That was my word. My guidance. My divine intervention to take my leave and move to the next chapter in my life.

My desert paradise, full of the blessings God had in store for me, was waiting. I was determined not to look like what I had been through. I was trusting God to enlarge my territory, to find real friendship and love in a relationship, to travel, to be prosperous and leave a legacy for my children and grands, to gain new friends, and to continue to impact the young and seasoned folks positively and to have the privilege to cross paths with, acquire wisdom from, and to enjoy new experiences (both spiritually and physically). I was trusting God to win. To be victorious!

Well, I had imagined building a ranch on the 40 acres of land God had allowed me to purchase and maintain after our divorce as part of the property settlement in AZ. I would build on 20 acres and leave the rest to my children and grandchildren.

If my husbands could walk away from me, I could let them go. I had to question, *"Were they God's best for me or just my manifested pathological demonstration of trauma bonding?"* They seemed to have the same toxic behaviors associated with alcohol, cocaine, anger, abandonment issues, poor mother and son relationships, infidelity, poor financial acuity, not emotionally mature or intelligent, looking outside themselves to fill what was missing in their soul. I was through dragging men to church. Unknowingly, they became projects for me as I attempted to save them and help them to help themselves. Each resented this help at times because either my help was behaviorally dismissed, or I was told, "I am not one of your clients."

At times, my husbands would act out as though I was competing with them and or resented that I was competent. To their credit and/or to my needs from childhood, I did feel cared for by their acts of service I received. Things like being handy in the home, taking my clothes to the cleaner, ensuring I looked well-dressed when going out, verbalizing I looked good in my attire, doing some household chores, being close to me in social settings. These things satisfied my feeling of being affirmed, being a woman.

I knew other men friends complimented my two husbands for having a woman who was respected and carried herself in a manner worthy of our spiritual and social status in the community. Some progress was made in my work and in their willingness to see problem areas and make modifications in their life and relationships. However, I certainly knew after these relationships that my "picker" was off center. I chose to forgive and give grace.

What is for me is for me.

"For I know the plans I have for you, declares the LORD, plans for welfare and not for evil, to give you a future and a hope."
Jeremiah 29:11 ESV

With the separation from my second husband, there was still a lesson that needed to be learned. I regarded my wedding vows with importance. I didn't want to have another failure of a marriage. I reflected on my behavior; I wanted to give this marriage 100 percent effort. There were no children involved except through my first marriage. They were older and I, clearly and age appropriately, shared the dynamics of the family and what was happening within the family.

After several months, my husband and I discussed domestic violence, and he was ordered to receive individual counseling as well as couples counseling. There were several underlying childhood traumas, diagnosis that had gone unaddressed throughout his life. Not to mention drug and alcohol and infidelity issues also. He was a semi functional hot mess for real. I was the caregiver working on him as a project with some love thrown in. Oddly enough I didn't feel fear of him; it was more sadness.

When it was time to move, I chose to only take a few items. My mother helped me pack some items as Arthur laid in the master bedroom. I asked him to help move some heavier things. He did. The home no longer felt like our home as he had his mistress in and out of the house and she was so bold as to purposely leave their card playing score sheets in our China hutch and other personal items. He had violated the sanctity of our marriage and physical home. I left the house, the BMW, and all the furnishings with him, including my precious written memories, pictures, and other personal items.[11]

Prior to my pulling off to Arizona, he did note it would be a long drive and asked me to telephone him upon arriving safely in Arizona. I agreed to do so. I asked God, in the name of Jesus, to be my front, side, and rear guard and give me traveling mercies for this leap of faith. Amen. I was ready to hit the road. I had my triple A road maps, a sense of adventure, good common sense, and most importantly, peace and a relaxed time schedule to accomplish my goal.

I planned to drive during the day, stopping at interesting locations to explore. I would get a motel room at dusk to pray and thank God for keeping me safe along the way. I had peaceful sleep and was ready to get an early prayerful start the next morning.

I documented my three-day solo journey from Pennsylvania to Glendale, Arizona. I contacted my apartment complex while in Flagstaff and informed them that I would be arriving in the Phoenix area in approximately three and a half hours. I was informed my apartment would be ready upon my arrival. God kept me. Hallelujah! It was a determined, safe, wonderful, peaceful drive. A divinely inspired pioneered relocation for this little country girl.

I never could have made it without you Jesus. And now that I have arrived in my Paradise, I can honestly say it was worth the wait! God has surrounded me with a church family, friends, and has provided me the opportunity to travel within the USA and abroad. His promises never fail, and He does make all things new. It is amazing how a 70+ year old can still have so much life left and the desire to keep going.

My Mission Statement 11/2008

"And the Lord's servant must not quarrel; Instead, He(she) must Be kind to everyone, able to teach, not resentful. Those who oppose him(her) must gently instruct, in the hope that God will grant them repentance leading them to a knowledge of the truth, and that they will come to their senses, and escape from the trap of the devil, who has taken them hostage."
2 Timothy 2:24-26 NIV

Evita and Verilyn

**Some of my Arizona Sister Tribe
(From Left to Right) Linda M., Christine T.,
Karen C., Karen A., Brenda T., Verilyn**

CHAPTER 18

God's Promises

I was born in Louisiana and transported to the mountainous, enclosed four-season state of Pennsylvania. The desert seemed like it was calling my name. It registered in my mind that it was my paradise. Come hell or high water, I had decided upon retirement; it was the place for me. I wanted to taste it for myself, learn to play golf, and I could always return to Pennsylvania if it didn't work out.

I drove solo to Arizona with the help of God and through his promises. He has restored all and added more than I left behind in Pennsylvania. I began looking to buy my home about two years after living in Glendale. I purposely slept on an air mattress and had very little furniture in my apartment so that I could save enough money for a down payment.

After two years, I found a southwest style home, stucco and tile roof, through a wonderful realtor. Because our divorce was not final, my husband made purchasing this home very difficult. I needed his signature on a document that waived any ownership or liability for this home, but he abstained from signing it. Again, I needed to use patience and prayer, so I prayed consistently and promised God that if he would allow my husband to go ahead and sign the waiver prior to our divorce, I would offer my home to women who needed a place to live for a certain amount of time. They could rent a bedroom from me. And God came through. My husband signed the paperwork, and I was able to purchase the home! And yes, eventually the divorce from Arthur was final.

Since arriving in Arizona, God has given me three opportunities to provide a bedroom for women. One of those women is Brianna, a young girl I met when she was 8 years old. Her adopted mother, Rose, is a missionary from Belize. I met Rose and Brianna when they were home on furlough. Upon visiting Fresh Start Church in 2008, I sat beside Rose and asked questions about the church and the pastor. Rose invited me to sit with her anytime we were both there. I joined this church and went on my first mission trip to Africa with this church. When Brianna turned 18, she and her child came to the USA for a better life. Rose and I have remained friends.

Here is a testimony from Brianna S., who has been a wonderful help to me.

Humble Beginnings

> *I was once a victim of domestic abuse. It got to the point of me being thrown out of a moving vehicle on the side of the freeway with my child. I was lost as to where I was and who I could contact for help. I was led to call Verilyn, and, by divine grace, she was just a couple of blocks away. She was able to pick us up and when I explained the situation, she asked if I would like to stay with her for a while. There, my daughter*

and I flourished, and I finally started to get back on my feet. I am grateful for Verilyn's kindness and sensitivity to the Spirit.

Brianna

God is great and greatly to be praised. I bask in the bright sunshine as a result of living in the Valley of the Sun (Son). I love the smell of rain and watching the Haboo (dust storms) that occur rolling over the desert, roads and homes. I have healthy fear and, so far, have not been stranded in one of those dust storms. Again, how amazing is God through nature. I love the wide-open spaces where I can see, for miles, the little hills and watch the rain fall from the heavens still on a bright shiny day. My soul and spirit just soar. I love the feeling of freedom in those moments. No limits, no boundaries. I love the majestic artistry of God as he paints the daily sunrises and sunsets. I love the breezes that cool me on a blistering hot day or feel like the heat from the inferno of hell holds me in its clutches when breathing in the hot air. The breezes cause the trees and palms leaves to flutter and bounce as if they are waving to all who watch them.

I am a grass roots kind of girl. I love and get great energy and satisfaction from direct service. I hate paperwork, but it is a necessary evil when writing reports for my clients and writing treatment plans.

I continued to work in Behavioral Health Care, purchased a home, and met wonderful believer friends. While traveling the world, I met a wonderful, kind man who loves me and has been a friend and companion. God continues to set me in a great group of believing women. I love that the Black couples and single ladies I have met here are financially secure and enjoy their relationships. All are purposed to enjoy life and leisure to the fullest. My heart is warmed as I see Black seasoned couples holding hands, loving each other. Society would have us believe that Black loving marriages are near zero percent. The devil is a liar. Most are transplants from other states.

When I was on a mission trip with Fresh Start Church, my brother, Al, received a diagnosis of Lupus and Kidney Disease. He passed away in 2010. Since residing in AZ, I have needed and gotten the opportunity / privilege to be a caregiver for my mom who had Dementia until her transition at 98 years old. She passed in 2019. My brother, Jay, transitioned in 2020 via a motorcycle crash in California.

I have also had the opportunity to be a caregiver for my only (and favorite) daughter for a few years until she moved back to Harrisburg. My daughter is diagnosed as schizophrenic, and I'm still praying continuously for her healing and stability. My daughter, while living with me, was also a great help to my mom and her grandmother. She has since returned to live on her own in Pennsylvania and has her ups and downs while remaining stable; but God is able to keep her. It is so amazing how God works to restore balance and right relations in our lives. Since my daughter has been living on her own, she was placed in a position of caregiving for her father for a few months after he was diagnosed with dementia and kicked out of his apartment. I encouraged her to ask questions and enjoy whatever time she had with her dad as he would engage in risky behaviors and walk off to go to the bar. Tomorrow is not promised.

My only (and favorite) son has been a rock for his family, me and his sister. He has grown into a leader; a wonderful, nurturing, hardworking man who I am very proud of. Since his father was not there for him or his sister in their childhood, there were men in the church who stepped up to be positive role models and to encourage him. So grateful for them. Dustin ushered their dad to his final resting place in death. He was one of 6 siblings, and he was placed in the role of burying his dad, an Army veteran, in 2024 without any assistance from his siblings.

"Honor your father and your mother, so that you may live long in the land the Lord your God is giving you."
Exodus 20:12

"Children's children are crowns to the aged, and parents are the pride of their children."
Proverbs 17:6

"I can do all this through him who gives me strength."
Philippians 4:13 NIV

Mother to Son
By Langston Hughes [12]

Well, son, I'll tell you:
Life for me ain't been no crystal stair.
It's had tacks in it,
And splinters,
And boards torn up,
And places with no carpet on the floor—
Bare.
But all the time
I'se been a-climbin' on,
And reachin' landin's,
And turnin' corners,
And sometimes goin' in the dark
Where there ain't been no light.
So boy, don't you turn back.
Don't you set down on the steps
'Cause you finds it's kinder hard.
Don't you fall now—
For I'se still goin', honey,
I'se still climbin',
And life for me ain't been no crystal stair.

Mama Louise with Carol, Al, Jay, Verilyn

My only and favorite son, Dustin, with his father

My only and favorite daughter, Danielle, touching her dad's final resting place. He was also a veteran.

CHAPTER 19

The Crossroads of Memory and Hope

I miss my siblings. None of them reached the age of 70. Carol was 48, Al was 61, and Jay was 66 upon their transition into eternal rest. Carol is buried just outside Carlisle, PA with her husband, Terry. Mom and Al are buried side by side in Harrisburg. Jay is buried in Indian Town Gap Military Cemetery outside of Harrisburg. I have chosen to be ready when the Lord calls me home and to be laid to rest with Al and Mom. I choose to be prepared. In looking back and evaluating life, I have realized a few things that have created the crossroads of memory and hope.

Our family was always a little on the outside of the community where we lived in Pennsylvania. We were included to some degree, but we all walked our own paths in life. Most of the primary families in Shippensburg were interrelated somewhere along their family lines, so that made clique. The Canaan's could weave in and out of various relationships and not be dependent or enmeshed; it appeared we could get along, go along without losing our family core identity, according to the comfortability level of each of us.

In the midst of all this, I was reminded continually how the responsibilities of caregiving and the rituals of farewell stretch across generations, touching each member of the family in their own unique way. There were days when my hands were busy—signing papers, making arrangements, listening to doctors, or simply holding the hand of someone I loved—and nights when my mind wandered through a maze of memories, worries, and half-spoken prayers. I often found myself marveling at the quiet strength of those around me— or my mother, whose resilience carried her through loss upon loss. These moments became sacred, woven with both sorrow and unexpected grace.

There are moments in life when the boundary between physical and the spiritual seems to dissolve, when the passage of a loved one lays bare the profound mystery of existence and departure. The memory of those final days, the waiting, the anticipation, the heartbreak—these remain etched upon my soul. In that sterile hospital room, time itself seemed suspended, as if the world was holding its breath with me. Each silent hour underscored the fragility of the human body and the resilience of the spirit. I realized that every goodbye is also an invocation of memory, a plea for understanding, and a hope that love endures beyond the visible world.

My Sister, Carol

My sister passed away after spending several months in and out of the hospital. Her transplanted kidney had failed, and dialysis was no longer effective. In conclusion, her body organs had begun turning on themselves. Eventually, she was admitted to the ICU for a couple of months. My niece Camille and I were in the Harrisburg hospital waiting room when Carol suddenly had an episode, and staff worked to revive her.

Camille and I waited anxiously in the waiting room, praying after being told by the doctors that we couldn't visit her. After what felt like much longer than an hour, we learned she had passed away. I'd shared a wonderful conversation with her days earlier. Seeing her then, I realized her eyes had lost their spark—the breath of life was gone. At that moment, I understood deeply how vital the Holy Spirit is in giving us light and life. God allowed me to see how the spirit is so significant to the physical. No more suffering, my sister. You fought the good fight. Farewell my sister. We will meet again.

Yet even as I navigated that uncertain space between hope and grief, I found myself holding tightly to fragments of conversation, the echo of a laugh, the lingering warmth of a hand in mine. There was a sacredness in those quiet moments, as if the hospital walls themselves bore silent witness to the invisible transfer of care, love, and worry from one generation to the next.

Looking back, I can see how every glance and every gentle assurance was not only for my sister, but for myself—a way of **gathering strength**, of preparing for the eventual letting go. It was in those days that I discovered grief is not a single, overwhelming wave, but a steady tide that shapes the landscape of our lives, carving out places for remembrance alongside sorrow. The words left unspoken, the reconciliations made in whispers or gestures, these too became vessels for our love.

Days passed in a haze of waiting, acceptance slowly threading itself through the ache. In those unfamiliar hours, I realized that loving someone through their final journey is as much an act of courage as it is of tenderness. There is a fierce beauty in standing watch, in promising to carry forward the stories, the wisdom, and the hopes entrusted to us.

And so, as the veil between worlds thinned and the hospital faded into memory, I stepped forward into the new shape of my life, changed but not alone, carrying with me the blessings and burdens of family, and the unwavering conviction that love endures, even as the forms it takes are transformed by loss.

Through every vigil and tearful conversation, I came to see caregiving not just as a duty, but as a final act of devotion—a way to honor those we have loved with presence and steadfastness, even as they prepared to slip beyond our sight or having an unexpected leave. There is a quiet heroism in the daily acts of care: the soft encouragement offered to a weary soul, the dignity preserved in small gestures, the forgiveness extended at the edge of parting. Life, in its fragile beauty, demanded that I bear witness not only to endings, but to the fullness of what came before.

And when loss arrived, as it inevitably does, I found that grief was not just an emptiness, but also a vessel—one that could hold the weight of gratitude and the glow of shared moments. In this way, love lingered, not as a shadow, but as a sustaining light, guiding me through the darkness and into a place where remembrance itself offered a quiet kind of healing.

I am grateful for the individuals who have been part of my journey, as well as those whose paths I have crossed. While I acknowledge that not every experience was ideal, each encounter provided valuable lessons. Upon reflection, I recognize that some relationships have been lost over time, particularly due to periods of estrangement within our family. Nonetheless, these experiences have contributed to my personal and professional growth.

My Brother, Al

During a 2010 mission trip to Africa, I had the opportunity to write my brother Al's name in the wet cement of a corner post at one of the tabernacles being constructed for training individuals in preaching. While abroad, I learned from our mission team leader that he had passed away a few days before our scheduled return to the United States. His family decided to wait until I could come home, preserving his remains so I could see him. He had experienced complications from Lupus, with ineffective dialysis, issues following a hip replacement, and significant pain, like Carol's experience. No more suffering my Al. I am so proud of how you turned your life around and took on the responsibilities of raising your children and being there for them. So proud of you and I miss you teasing me about all my many names. I wish to inform you that I have gained valuable knowledge and insight through the experiences associated with each of my names. Let your spirit commune with our motherland ancestors. ASE.

My Brother, Jay

When my mother was put into Hospice, I wrote to Jay, who was living in Bakersfield, California. There had been a lot of hurt and division between me and Jay, and I wanted to seek his forgiveness and give him mine. I wanted him to know about Mom and to give him the opportunity to come see her. Everyone deserves to know what's happening with their mother, no matter what else has transpired. I sent him a letter and he called me to let me know things were okay. He wasn't much of a talker, but he always had things going on inside his head and heart. He said he would come and see Mom, and then he asked if I would take care of him should something happen, and I said yes. I had no idea that my "yes" would be needed sooner than later.

One evening, I received a phone call from California State troopers who told me my brother had passed away due to a motorcycle accident going around the mountains in California. They found the letter I had sent, so they knew my Mom and I were in Arizona. They asked if I could come and claim his remains.

I was used by God to place him in his final resting place in 2020. I was not able to see his body because he was so badly torn up. God orders our steps. He is the author and the finisher of our lives. God, you allowed everything to go very smoothly, and I thank you for that. Jay is buried in the Indiantown gap military cemetery with full honors.

Family Caregiver

God had plans and positioned me to be the family caregiver, steward, guard, and in charge of the physical bodily house of my mother, brothers, and sister, as they were moving through this part of Zion as their spirit was waning. The ache of missed goodbyes lingers and are sharper than words can express.

I recall searching Mom's face for signs of recognition, for a flicker of the vitality I once knew. Instead, I found a staring and a stillness that signaled a journey already begun. In addition, I saw Carol with a dullness in her cold, still eyes; a crossing over to a place I could not follow. Not yet.

Even with all the responsibilities, heartbreaks, and reconciliations, the weight of these memories sits gently on my shoulders—a collection of stories and silences I carry forward. In the stillness after loss, I often find myself reflecting on the invisible threads that connect us, even when we are scattered or estranged. There is an unspoken lineage of love and pain passed on through gestures, sacrifices, and sometimes just a simple word left unsaid.

Through the process of letting go, I've come to understand the limits of our understanding, the unpredictable paths that draw family together and apart. Each call, each letter, each meeting at the hospital or at a gravesite became more than just a moment in time—they became markers along the winding roads of our shared existence. I hold onto the belief that, in forgiveness and remembrance, we write a new story for those who come after, and for ourselves.

Grief, with all its weight and mystery, found me wandering through memories—some fragmented, some vivid, each threaded together in the tapestry of our family's journey. There are moments, even now, when I close my eyes and see the faces of those I've loved, hear the soft cadence of voices once so familiar, and feel, for a fleeting instant, that warmth of togetherness we sometimes managed to create despite the misunderstandings and distances.

In the quiet spaces between sorrow and gratitude, I realize how each loss has shaped my heart, how the echoes of each farewell linger in the corners of my spirit. The pain of separation is softened, somehow, by the knowledge that forgiveness was offered and received, that bonds—though stretched—were not entirely severed. I carry with me all the lessons, the regrets, the small triumphs of reconciliation, and the silent prayers for peace that have sustained me through the darkest nights.

Now, as I look ahead, I find comfort in the rituals of remembrance: lighting a candle, whispering a name, sharing a story with those who remain. The journey is not over. Love endures, and hope quietly persists, leading me onward—one step at a time—toward a future where the presence of those

I've lost is not absence, but a gentle light guiding me home. Mission accomplished for my immediate sibling generation ...good steward.

Proverbs 16:1-4 The Message says,

> *"Mortals make elaborate plans, but God has the last word humans are satisfied with whatever looks good. God probes for what is good. put God in charge of your work then what you have planned will take place. God made everything with a place and purpose even the wicked are included but for judgment."*
> *"We plan the way we want to live, but only*
> *God makes us able to live it."*
> *Proverbs 16:9*

I was underestimated in formative years, but I'm still coming out, stepping up, and walking in the lighted path that is my purpose. To God be the glory! Hallelujah!

It appears that I have blossomed into the bold, good natured, joyful persona that everyone else encountered in my lifetime experienced. I had to clear my internal lens and see she has been there all along. Freedom! I see me now. I am that I am.

Upon recent reflection, I recognize that I have developed into the confident, positive, and joyful individual described by those who have known me. By shifting my perspective, I have come to understand that these qualities have always been present within me. **I now have a clear sense of self-awareness and acceptance. I know who I am and whose I am.**

Standing at the crossroads of memory and hope, I understand now that our stories aren't just records of pain or triumph— they are lanterns lighting the path for each step forward.

Every trial, every joy, every silent prayer has shaped me into someone who can both honor the past and embrace the future. I am learning to cherish the mosaic of my life—the shattered fragments as well as the pieces polished by grace—seeing how each fits together in a pattern only time and faith could reveal.

There is a quiet power in reclaiming myself after seasons of doubt and loss. I move forward, not as someone untouched by grief, but as one who has let sorrow carve out deeper wells of compassion within. The laughter I share now is richer for the tears that have watered it; the courage I find is rooted in the moments when I faced the darkness and chose to keep walking.

In this space of newfound freedom, I am grateful for the ancestors, the mentors, the friends, and even the struggles that have **shaped my becoming**. I walk with purpose, not because the journey has been easy, but because it has taught me how resilient hope can be. Each sunrise brings a fresh invitation to live boldly, to speak truth, and to love without reserve. The legacy I carry is not only one of endurance but of radiant possibility—a testament that even after storms, the heart can bloom again.

So I step out, whole and seen—guided by the light within, trusting that the same hand that led me through shadows will continue to chart my course. I embrace the fullness of who I am, whispering gratitude for the journey and anticipation for all that is yet to unfold.

CHAPTER 20

My Testimony

"Keep your lives free from the love of money and be content with what you have, because God has said, never will I leave you; never will I forsake you. So we say with confidence, 'The Lord is my helper; I will not be afraid.'"
Hebrews 13:5-6 NIV

"When the advocate comes, whom I will send to you from the Father—the spirit of truth who goes out from the father—he will testify about me. And you also must testify, for you have been with me from the beginning."
John 15:26, John 3:16 NIV

"The Lord himself goes before you and will be with you; he will never leave you nor forsake you. Do not be afraid; do not be discouraged."
Deuteronomy 31:8 NIV

God is a sovereign God. God of love. Our Father in heaven, thank you for choosing me. Jesus is the living word of God,

God's son, my redeemer, savior, and friend. The Holy Ghost is 1/3 of the Godhead, my comforter, counselor, my help, and a gift for all believers.

The Holy Spirit is a personal source of a personal testimony and must reveal the supernatural power of God. Jesus can guide us in our decisions. He talks with us and tells me I am His own. He is my protector and help. The Bible helped me to know that "God's got this" with whatever I am going through. Just trust God. He is in control.

We need to be faithful because God is faithful and trustworthy. He keeps his promises and commandments. Stay hopeful and at peace in this world. In my decisions, God is first in my life. God is my source. Emmanuel is with me always. God's plan is to not harm me but to give me sanity. I am to be a receiver of his good things.

I also know that trials / lessons will come, but I need to do the next right thing according to God's word, prayer, and urgings from the Holy Spirit. I need to keep praising God in all things, at all times, having a spirit of gratitude to be open in the spirit and maintaining a personal relationship / fellowship with Him, because I don't know where I would be without God, except dead and in my literal and spiritual grave. I have to be submissive in my walk with God, dump the arrogance, myths, distrust, acting like I know it all, trying to know what God knows and "make it make sense to my small mind." Thus ensued my seeking after God for myself.

Through so many trials and snares I have already come; I know God was with me and He was going to lovingly protect me and develop me. I wanted to give my children a lasting connection and foundation, just as I have had. I became very active in the church, Bible study, Sunday school, teaching children's church, ushering, serving as trustee, and attending business meetings. I could never sing, but I make a joyful noise whenever I have the opportunity.

This is just the beginning, but God has protected and blessed me, put righteous people and not so righteous people in my life. I would like to highlight the goodness of God by His sending me two beautiful, kind, nurturing spiritual mothers who have played a vital part in my life.

Anna guided me to my first state job in Pennsylvania and her counsel regarding my surrender to Jesus the Christ, men, and being a wife. She also helped me to make a house a home and to keep striving to improve my material and financial status. Anna was also a well-dressed put-together Black woman. She loved her fur stoles, suits, and beautiful shoes. We had such honest, straight-forward discussions and great laughter.

Rosa gravitated toward me for some reason. She would sit on the opposite side of the Goodwin Memorial church from me. She would frequently interact with me and offer a hug. During my pregnancy, she inquired about my well-being and reminded me to take care of myself. Rosa was a tall, big bosom, classy, well-dressed woman of few words, yet very nurturing. We had very girly, straight-to-the-point-no-chaser discussions and laughs. She was the friend who drove me to the hospital when I needed surgery on my ears.

I have learned to have my voice and my boundaries. I have loosed a lot of anger and feelings of inadequacies and have learned to just be myself. I still give and get love in return. It is so wonderful to have balance to enjoy myself alone in my house and in my own body and still have a cherished bounty of beautiful people in my life. And it is a joy to open my home to the women God brings to stay for a season because of the promise I made to Him! As He is generous with me, I want to be the same with Him.

I have been saved and kept by God so many times in all my Blackness. Through all circumstances, I am more than a conqueror in Christ Jesus. **I have had to summon up my God-strength.** He kept me safe when I was driving with a seizure, not killing anyone else. When I received confirmation of my journey to Arizona from a prophetess. After the death of all my siblings and parents. He kept me safe when I had a judgmental heart and when I was hurt by the people of God. I am not a believer in those people; I keep my focus on God and all He has provided for me beyond measure in these 70+ years.

My walk today is, *"Holy Spirit, speak to my heart, if I don't hear from you, I don't know what to do. Speak to my heart. Help me find this or that. Should I do this or that? Give me wisdom and discernment. Help me to be bold in you, Jesus."*

I have seen angels and demons in people. My spirit has been convicted to apologize for this or that, for my direct prickly tone at times, etc. I am still under construction! Walking in His light in the garden. Thank you, Jesus! I am grateful, grateful, grateful.

As long as Moses held his hands up, the Israelites were winning, but as soon as he let them fall, the enemy began to win. Doing God's will, I don't always have to be in the front. I am not needing to be seen, but obeying and trusting God in service is just learning to hear where to stand and be courageous to His plan. What I do need to do, though, is to **always and forever summon my God-strength,** and I hope you will do the same.

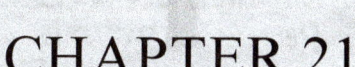

CHAPTER 21

Tapping Into the Strength of God

Bless the LORD! Thank you, JESUS! In 2025, I am alive! I am still winning! God has restored all that I left behind and multiplied the blessings! God be Glorified!

"But seek first the kingdom of God and his righteousness,
and all these things will be added to you."
Matthew 6:33 ESV

"No weapons fashioned against you shall succeed, and
you shall refute every tongue that rises against you in
judgement. This is the heritage of the servants of the Lord
and their vindication from me, declares the LORD."
Isaiah 54:14 ESV

"Trust in the Lord with all your heart and lean not
on your own understanding; In all your ways submit
to him, and he will make your paths straight."
Proverbs 3:5-6 NIV

"In their heart's, humans plan their course,
but the LORD establishes their steps."
Proverbs 16:9 NIV

Praise God at all times.
"I will never leave you nor forsake thee. The Lord is my
helper; I will not fear; what can man do to me?"
Hebrews 13:5-6 KJV

How to TAP INTO THE STRENGTH OF GOD [13]

John Piper suggests 5 steps to finding strength in God.
Introducing:

- A. Admit that you can do nothing (acknowledge the task)
- P. Pray for God's help for the task at hand
- T. Trust a particular promise of God's help. Then, in that faith (trusting in the promise of the supply in the specific situation)
- A. Act, and finally,
- T. Thank God for the help received

"Surely goodness and mercy(love) shall follow me all the days
of my life, and I will dwell in the house of the LORD forever."
Psalm 23:6 NIV

"I will bless the Lord at all times and his praise shall
continually be in my mouth. I sought the Lord, and he
heard me, and delivered me from all my fears."
Psalm 34:1 KJV

"Enter his gates with thanksgiving, and into his courts
with praise; be thankful unto him and bless his name."
Psalm 100:4 KJV

"May my prayers be set before you like incense; may the lifting up of my hands be like evening sacrifice. Set a guard over my mouth LORD."
Psalm 141:2 NIV

EPILOGUE

I enjoy meeting new people and having conversations, sharing opinions and God. I am starting to learn new things. I love old movies, including cowboy movies, and I wanted to be in one. I had head shots taken and actively researched opportunities. I went to various production companies who were requesting extras. I don't need to be up front and or a primary actor. Being in the background is exciting, and to be in the movie is the goal. This is an exciting past time for me as a retiree and wanting to be adventuresome in my life. I know that many times the role of extras is left on the cutting floor during the editing of a film.

And now, premiering in 2024, was the year of achieving my goal of being an extra in the movie called *"Destiny, The Greater the Struggle, the Greater the Destiny"* written by Esther Morgan with Arts Touching Lives. It is a faith-based movie.

I also love period movies, and I had the opportunity to join a group of the Buffalo Soldiers in AZ for about 3 years.

This took me back to the times of slavery. I loved representing a Black female with high societal status, representing a Lady of the Regiment. I was able to attend city wide parades, re-enact and perform in schools and city events and churches. I dressed in 1865 period clothing. I chose to re-enact an intriguing Black female historical character of Mary E. Bowser during the Civil War period.

She was born a slave in 1840 and became a Union spy. She was one of the intelligence spies who worked as a domestic. Ms. Bowser is said to have had a photographic memory when she assumed the identity of an illiterate slave woman and found a place as a house servant in the confederate White House, Richmond. She was able to gain access to lists of troop movements reports on the location of union prisoners' military strategies and treasury reports. She passed the information along to the union until she was discovered and fled Richmond near the end of the war. She received her education at the Quaker School for Negroes in Philadelphia.

Elizabeth Van Lew freed Mary Bowser who was a staunch abolitionist in Virginia. Bowsers bravery and cunning played a pivotal role in the Union's victory. She is recognized and her name is placed into the Military Intelligence Hall of Fame in 1995. A copy of the document is in Fort Huachuca Army base in Cochise, AZ.

Verilyn in the Buffalo Soldiers

Destiny Movie Premiere

A BLESSING FOR YOU

I wrote this in my journal 6/26/2022 as a reference as I was reviewing prior trials and tribulations that He has already brought me through, as well as the privileged opportunities to be of service!

Thank you, Father God, thank you, Jesus my savior and friend! I wanted God to speak to my heart.

> *"**The God of Glory** – how blessed is God! And what a blessing he is! He's the father of our master Jesus Christ and takes us to the high places of blessing in him.*
>
> *He laid down earth's foundations, he had us in mind, and has settled on us as the focus of his love to be made whole and holy by his love.*
>
> *Long, long ago, he decided to adopt us into his family through Jesus Christ.*
>
> *He wanted us to enter into the celebration of his lavish gift-giving by the hand of his beloved son.*

*Because of the sacrifice of the Messiah, his blood poured out on the altar of the cross, we're a free people, free of penalties and punishments chalked up by all our misdeeds and not just barely free either. **Abundantly free!***

*He thought of everything, provided for everything we could possibly need, letting us in on the plans he took such delight in making he set it all out before us in Christ, a long range plan in which everything would be brought together and summed up in him, everything in deepest heaven, everything on planet earth, it's in Christ that we find out who we are and what we are living for long before we first heard of Christ and got our hopes up **he had his eye on us**, had designs on us for glorious living, part of the overall purpose he is working out in everything and everyone.*

It's in Christ that you once you heard the truth and believed it, this is the message of your salvation, found yourselves home free, signed, sealed, and delivered by the Holy Spirit. This down payment from God is the first installment on what's coming a reminder that we'll get everything God has planned for us.

*A praising and glorious life, I ask the God of our master Jesus Christ the God of glory to make you intelligent and discerning and knowing him personally, your eyes focus and clear so that you can see exactly what it is he is calling you to do. Grasp the immensity of this glorious way of life he has for his followers, oh the utter extravagance of his work in us who trust him, endless energy, **boundless strength,** all this energy issues from Christ: God raised him from the dead and set him on a throne and deep heaven in charge of running the universe everything from galaxies to governments. No name and no power exempt from his rule. And not just for the time being but forever. He is in charge of it all, has the final word on everything.*

At the center of all this Christ rules the church. The church you see is not peripheral to the world; the world is peripheral to the church. The church is Christ's body in which he speaks and acts by which he fills everything with his presence. I rest in his presence and strength!"

Ephesians 1:3-23 The Message

NOTES

Chapter 1
[1] More about this in Chapter 17.

Chapter 2
[2] To this day, I give underwear and things people need rather than what they may want.

Chapter 3
[3] We still reminisce about that when I visit her in California.

Chapter 4
[4] Paul was my favorite member of the band.

[5] J was good in baseball and sports. Really, all four of us were good at sports.

Chapter 5
[6] I think these public speaking episodes helped me be less nervous to speak in front of people, and I'm also comfortable expressing my opinion on a topic. Thank you, Dad.
[7] Those feelings were repressed in me for a long time, and they would eventually find their way out in a rage.

Chapter 9

[8] My lifelong friends are Ollievita, Senia, Darcy, Bunnie, Evelyn, Bettice, Cheryl, Sharon, Denise, Anita, Bettie, Ronnie, Donna, and Shar, in no particular order. We have been friends for 50 years. Some (Denise, Sharon) have gained their wings and have transitioned to eternal rest but not forgotten. This is my tribe, and they are each godly, divined, educated, supportive, affluent, and hilariously funny.

Chapter 10

[9] I also helped Dave acquire a Recreational Supervisor position in Corrections when they began expanding prisons into the coal mining areas!

Chapter 14

[10] My brother, Al, had Lupus and transitioned in 2010 during my church mission trip to Bioko Island Malabo, Equatorial Guinea, Africa. Our mission: To build a Bible school for all people.

Chapter 17

[11] When I started pulling together information to write this book, I again realized how much I had left behind. But my God is a restorer.

Chapter 18

[12] *The Collected Works of Langston Hughes* (University of Missouri Press (BkMk Press), 2002)

Chapter 21

[13] John Piper @John Piper founder and teacher of Desiring God and Chancellor of Bethlehem College and Seminary. Article "Desiring God" September 2, 2014

ABOUT THE AUTHOR

Verilyn Jackson-Downing is a woman of God, holding a Master of Science degree as a Community Counselor, and a Bachelor of Science degree as a Recreation Instructor. She is a mentor, group facilitator, veteran, and has a motivational personality.

She was certified as a National Certified Counselor, a Certified Allied Addiction Practitioner, and a Licensed Professional Counselor in Pennsylvania. She has experience working in behavioral health care, private counseling services, criminal justice, adolescent sexual offenders / foster care services, domestic violence, drug and alcohol educational groups, and individual therapy. Verilyn has instructed state male prisoners in lifetime sports skills.

As a retiree, she teaches kindergarten-4th grade students reading skills. She serves in her church Prayer and Evangelism Ministry; sharing the word of God by praying with and for others to help encourage them through life's challenges.

Verilyn is a mother, grandmother, and friend. She supports praying with and for others, whether in public schools, in prison, or in private, to encourage them and to share Jesus Christ through all we encounter.

Verilyn continues to seek joy for her journey!

Contact information:
verilycanaan@gmail.com

Verilyn with Adult Children and Grandchildren

www.ingramcontent.com/pod-product-compliance
Lightning Source LLC
Chambersburg PA
CBHW071146120626
46546CB00006B/2144